6-29

PSYCHOLOGY

AND

INTERNATIONAL RELATIONS

Edited By

Gerald Sperrazzo
Georgetown University

Georgetown University Press
Washington, D. C.

JX
1255
.S9
1964

# PREFACE

For the first time in the history of the world, mankind has developed the capacity to annihilate itself. Never before has this potential level of destruction been achieved. Man has labored through wars and has learned to live with them. But this may be a different war with such destructive powers that those left after the mass annihilation will truly be called the "living dead."

The advent of atomic energy brought us to an historical crossroad in determining the future of this planet. The energy discovered may be used either to enhance life and living conditions one hundred fold, or it can make history record the folly of man's incapacity to live harmoniously with man. The time has come to exert every measure of his genius to bring men to the conference table so that they may solve human problems in a human way. The alternatives of conflict among peoples are few. We must learn to understand each other and settle differences in a rational way, or the cry to aggression may lead to the most insuperable error of mankind.

The solutions to these problems are not available nor will time itself necessarily resolve human and international conflicts. They demand careful study, deep understanding, and a strong conviction that conflicts among peoples can be understood and ameliorated. To this end the behavioral scientist has been called upon to contribute his resources in maintaining peace, and in resolving conflicts.

The papers contained in this book were originally presented at the Symposium on Psychology and International Relations held at Georgetown University in June, 1964 as a part of its 175th Anniversary celebration. The purpose of the symposium was to bring together prominent behavioral scientists to present and discuss their views of the ways in which the behavioral scientist can contribute to this field.

The diversity of interest reflected in these papers was by design and not by accident. The selection of the participant was intended to reflect this diversity since there is no single path or point of view that is best suited for the behavioral scientist in his confrontation with the problem of understanding international behavior.

The existence of this book is due to many people but I wish to express my gratitude specifically to Rev. George H. Dunne, S. J., for sponsoring the symposium; to Rev. Brian A. McGrath, S. J., Academic Vice President, and Dr. Rocco Porreco, Dean of the Summer School, for support of this publication; and to Mr. Donald Cowan for his invaluable assistance during the symposium. Finally, to my wife Mary, and to my son Mark, I affectionately dedicate this volume.

Gerald Sperrazzo

Georgetown University
Washington, D. C.

CONTENTS

# A PSYCHOLOGICAL APPROACH TO INTERNATIONAL CONFLICT

Morton Deutsch
Columbia University

Ponder these examples:

The Korean war was started by a serious misjudgment of U.S. intentions. U.S. intentions were probably not clearly known to itself.

The Bay of Pigs invasion was based on a grossly inaccurate prediction of how the Cuban people would respond.

The Cuban crisis of 1962 was based on a Soviet misunderstanding of how the United States would react to the placement of missiles so close to our shores.

The only use of atomic weapons against human beings - the bombings of Hiroshima and Nagasaki - was based on miscalculation. These bombings, it has been concluded, "made no essential contribution to Japan's surrender without a last battle."[1]

It seems likely that if atomic bombs are ever again dropped on human beings they will be employed as a result of misjudgment, despair, or insanity during the course of international conflict. How can we manage conflict so that it does not foster either fatal illusions or dangerous misapprehensions? How can we control conflict so that it becomes a stimulus to constructive social change rather than a source of mutual defensiveness and hostility? These are the questions I shall address myself to in this paper.

Note that I do not presuppose that conflict and controversy can be or should be eliminated either among nations or among people. As a psychologist, as a husband, and as a father I am convinced that conflict is an inevitable part of social life. It is as desirable as it is inevitable. It prevents stagnation, it is the medium through which problems can be aired and solutions arrived at; it is the heart of social change. Our objective is not to create a world in which conflict is suppressed but rather a world in which it is civilized.

How do we make conflict lively rather than deadly? How do we eliminate or reduce the "cut-throat" character of cut-throat competition? How do we prevent or overcome distortions in social perception? These are questions to which there is, as now well-established, scientifically-verified knowledge. Yet there are "informed hunches" based upon a growing body of experience with intrapersonal quandaries, interpersonal controversies. marital quarrels, intergroup conflicts, labor-management disputes, community conflicts, political struggles, etc., which seem to suggest some general principles.

Let me indicate some of the general principles which I will be drawing up during my talk:

1. Genuine conflicts of interest are often exacerbated and made more difficult to resolve by hostile misperceptions.

2. The social psychological dynamics of conflict are such as to foster perceptions of one another which tend to perpetuate conflicts even after the initial basis of conflict has become irrelevant.

3. Many conflicts have their origins in misperceptions.

4. Conflict is more likely to be conducted within mutually acceptable procedures and rules in situations where the parties have less at stake in a particular conflict than they do in the ongoing relationship between them or in the community which has generated the rules for regulating conflict. As Roger Fisher of the Harvard Law School has put it, "If a country is going to be willing to lose a particular conflict rather than fight, it must perceive that its gains from existing and future international cooperation are greater than the loss it may suffer on this particular occasion."[2]

An implication of this fourth principle is that efforts to control conflict can be designed to affect either the stake in the conflict or the stake in the ongoing relations. The following two principles relate to the two kinds of stakes.

5. "Issue control," the deliberate effort to define the issues in conflict in such a way as to limit their scope, is one way of making a conflict more resolvable.

6. The development of cooperative bonds, the stimulation of the awareness of mutually facilitating interests, the promotion of superordinate, common allegiances and goals, the recognition of common principles, procedures and institutions - all of these tend to lead to the use of techniques of persuasion and mutual compromise rather than those of violence or deceit when an issue of conflict arises.

## Misperceptions Which Lead to or Exacerbate Conflict

I have suggested above that conflict may be initiated or enhanced by misperceptions. There are a number of reasons why perceptions may be distorted. I would like to consider with you some common causes of misperception, to illustrate the operation of each in international relations, and to indicate how these misperceptions can be counteracted or prevented.

1. The perception of any act is determined both by our perception of the act itself and by our perception of the context in which the act occurs. Thus, the statement, "You did that extremely well," will be perceived rather differently if a captain is saying it to a private than if a private is saying it to a captain.[3] The contexts of social acts are often not immediately given in perception and often they are not obvious. When the context is not obvious, we tend to assume a familiar context - i. e., the context which is most likely in terms of our own experience. Since both the present situations and past experiences of the actor and the perceiver may be rather different, it is not surprising that they will supply different contexts and interpret the same act quite differently. Misunderstandings of this sort, of course, are very likely when the actor and the perceiver come from rather different cultural backgrounds and they are not fully aware of these differences. The stock conversation of returning tourists consists of amusing or embarrassing anecdotes based upon misunderstandings of this sort.

Urie Bronfenbrenner's first-hand observations led him to conclude that the Soviets and Americans have a similar view of one an-

other; each says more or less the same things about the other.  For
example, each states: "they are the aggressors"; their government
exploits and deludes the people"; "the mass of their people is not
really sympathetic to the regime"; "they cannot be trusted"; "their
policy verges on madness, " etc. [4]

It is my contention that mutual distortions such as those described above arise, in part, because of an inadequate understanding
of the other's context.  Take, for instance, the view that "the mass of
their people are not really sympathetic to the regime. "  In effect, we
ask ourselves if Soviet citizens had the choice between (a) living in
Russia if it were like the United States with its high standard of living
and its political system of civil liberties,  and (b) living in the present
day Soviet Union, which would they choose?  We think the answer is
obvious, but isn't it clear that the question is wrong?  The relevant
comparison for them is between their past and their present or future:
their present and future is undoubtedly vastly superior to their past.
Similarly, the Soviet view is that a comparison between (a) Soviet
society with its full employment and expanding economy with (b) capitalism in a permanent depression crisis would favor the Soviet Union.
Perhaps it would, but is this the relevant comparison?

How can we prevent and overcome distortions and misunderstandings of this sort?  Obviously,  more communication, a great increase in interchanges of scholars, artists, politicians, tourists and
the like might be helpful.  However, I think we should take cognizance
of the findings of the vast body of research on intergroup contact:
casual contact of limited duration is more likely to support deeply
rooted distortions than remove them.  To have any important effect,
contact must be prolonged, functional, and intimate.

I suggest that the most important principle to follow in international communication on issues where there is controversy is one suggested by John Cohen and by Anatol Rapoport:  role reversal.  Acting
on this principle,  each side would be required to state the position of
the other side to the other side's complete satisfaction before either
side advocates its own position.  Certainly the procedure would not
eliminate conflict but it would help to eliminate misunderstanding.  It
forces one to place the other's action in a context which is acceptable
to the other and, as a consequence, prevents one from arbitrarily re-
jecting his position as unreasonable or badly motivated.

2. Our perceptions are very much influenced by our expectations and preconceptions.  Thus, a person who expects Negroes to be
aggressive is likely to perceive an altercation between a Negro and
White as having been initiated by the former.  Once a child has ac-
quired the reputation of being a trouble-maker,  there is a tendency to
connect him with unexplained trouble around the house, and a tendency
to continue to see him this way even after he has changed.  Similarly,
in international relations.  Our preconception is that Communist nations are aggressive, trouble-makers and that we are unprovocative,
peace-loving defenders of freedom.  With such different preconceptions
about their actions and our actions, it is hardly surprising that there
is a double standard in appraising Soviet and American actions.  Thus,

3

American college students have favorable reactions to such statements as: "The U.S. has established rocket bases close to the borders of Russia"; "The U.S. has frequently stated that its armaments are for defensive purposes and will not be used in a first strike against Russia"; "Leaders of the U.S. government have frequently called for liberation of the captive peoples in the Russian satellite nations." However, they have rather negative reactions when the statements are expressed as Russian actions - e.g., "Russia has established rocket bases close to the borders of the U.S."[5]

Our view of the Communists as "trouble-makers" leads us to perceive them as the root of international trouble - as though they were the instigators to the Viet Cong rebellion in Vietnam, as though they were the cause of the Castro revolution, as though they were sending more military equipment, military personnel, secret agents, etc. into Africa, Latin America, and Asia than we have been. The tendency to link communism in international trouble, of course, makes it difficult to accept the possibility that they might, after all, have some interests in international order. It inhibits us in our attempt to work out procedures for "fair competition" in the underdeveloped countries: we are convinced, before we try, that it would be doomed to failure.

3. Our perceptions of the external world are often determined indirectly by the information we receive from others rather than by our direct experiences. Human communication, like perception itself, is always selective. The perception of an event is usually less detailed, more abstract, and less complex than the event which is perceived; the communication about an event is also likely to be less detailed and less complex than its perception. The more human links there are in the communication of information about any event, the more simplified and distorted will be the representation of the event. Distortion in communication tends to take characteristic form: on the one hand, there is a tendency to accentuate the unusual, bizarre, controversial, deviant, violent, and unexpected; on the other hand, there is a tendency for communicators who are communicating to their superiors to communicate only that information which fits in with the preconceptions of their superiors.

If we examine our sources of information about international affairs, we see that they are particularly vulnerable to distorting influences. There are only a small number of American reporters in any country; they do not necessarily work independently of one another. They are under subtle pressure to report items which will catch the reader's interest and conform to their publisher's viewpoint. In a period of hostility between nations, these conditions are not conducive to getting a clear understanding of how events are perceived by the other side or a clear understanding of the other's frame of reference.

I suggest that we should recognize the dangers inherent in not perceiving the other side's point of view regularly. Recognizing these dangers, shouldn't we offer to make arrangements with the Soviet Union whereby we would each be enabled to present our own point of view over the other's radio and TV and in their leading newspapers? Suppose the Soviet leaders are afraid to participate on a reciprocating basis, should

4

we make the offer anyway? My answer is in the form of a question: do we have anything to lose by understanding their viewpoint as well as we can; wouldn't "truth squads" adequately protect us from deliberate attempts to mislead us?

4. Our perceptions of the world are often very much influenced by the need to conform to and agree with the perceptions of other people. Thus, in some communities it would be difficult for an individual to survive if he perceived Negroes as his social equals or if he perceived Communist China as having legitimate grievances against the United States. If he acted upon his perceptions he would be ostracized socially; if he conformed to the perceptions of other people without changing his own perceptions, so that they were similar to those prevalent in his community, he might feel little self-respect.

It is my impression that most social and political scientists, most specialists in international relations, most intellectuals who have thought about it, and many of our political leaders personally favor the admission of Communist China into the UN and favor our taking the initiative in attempting to normalize our relations with Communist China. Yet, conformity pressures keep silent most of us who favor such a change in policy. The strength of these conformity pressures in the United States on this issue has been so great that it has been difficult to think of Communist China or to talk about it in any terms except those which connote absolute, incorrigible evil.

How can we break through the veil of conformity and its distorting influences? Asch's[6] insightful studies of conformity pressures point the way. His studies reveal that when the monolithic social front of conformity is broken by even one dissenter, other potential dissenters feel freer to break with the majority. The lesson is clear: those who dissent must express their opinions so that they are heard by others. If they do so, they may find more agreement than they anticipate. France's action, in recognizing China and breaking through the veil of conformity imposed by the United States, may make us all freer.

5. A considerable body of psychological research[7] indicates that an individual attempts to perceive his environment in such a way it is consistent with his self-perception. If an individual feels afraid, he tends to perceive his world as frightening; if he feels hostile, he is likely to see it as frustrating or unjust; if he feels weak and vulnerable, he is apt to see it as exploitative and powerful; if he is torn by self-doubt and self-conflict, he will tend to see it as at odds with him. Not only does an individual tend to see the external world in such a way as to justify his feelings and beliefs but also so as to justify his behavior. If an individual is a heavy smoker, he is apt to perceive cigarette smoking as less injurious to health than a nonsmoker; if he drives a car and injures a pedestrian, he is likely to blame the pedestrian; if he invests in something (e. g., a munitions industry), he will attempt to justify and protect his investment. Morever, there is much evidence that an individual tends to perceive the different parts of his world as consistent with one another. Thus, if somebody likes you, you expect him to dislike someone who dislikes you. If somebody disagrees with you, you are likely to expect him to agree with someone who disagrees with you.

The danger of the pressure for consistency is that it often leads to an oversimplified black-white view of the world. Take, for instance, the notions that since the interests of the United States and the Soviet Union are opposed in some respects, we must be opposed to or suspicious of anything that the Communists favor and must regard any nation that desires friendly relations with the Soviet Union as opposed to the United States. If the Soviet Union is against colonialism in Africa, must we be for it? If nations in Latin America wish to establish friendly, commercial relations with the Communist nations, must we feel threatened? If Canada helps Communist China by exporting food to it, must we suspect its loyalty to us? Are nations which are not for us necessarily for the Communists? The notions expressed in affirmative answers to these questions are consistent with the view that the conflict between the United States and the Soviet Union (or China) can only be ended by total defeat for one or the other. But is it not possible that the conflict can be resolved so that both sides are better off than they are now? Recognition of this latter possibility may suggest that what benefits the Soviet Union does not necessarily harm us, and that nations with amicable relations with both the United States and China may be an important asset in resolving conflict.

What can we do to avoid the "consistency of little minds" and the rigidities of false pride? These dangers to accurate perception are the most likely when an individual feels under threat, when his self-esteem is at stake. I think in such circumstances it is prudent to seek the advice and counsel of trusted friends who are not so emotionally involved in the issues. Thus, I think it would be wise to consult with such nations as Brazil, France, and Great Britain on our policy toward Cuba and Communist China precisely because they do not have as deep an involvement with these countries as we do. Similarly, consultation with more or less neutral nations such as India, Sweden, Austria, and Nigeria might prevent us from developing an oversimplified view of the nature of our relations with the Soviet Union.

6. Ichheiser has described a mechanism, similar to that of projection, when leads to misunderstandings in human relations: the mote-beam mechanism. It consists in perceiving certain characteristics in others which we do not perceive in ourselves. Thus, the characteristics are perceived as though they were peculiar traits of the others and, hence, the differences between the others and ourselves are accentuated. Since the traits we are unable or unwilling to recognize in others are usually traits we consider to be undesirable, the mote-beam mechanism results in a view of the other as peculiarly shameful or evil. Thus, although many of us who live here in the North easily recognize the shameful racial discrimination and segregation in the South, we avoid a clear awareness of the pervasive racial discrimination in our own communities.

Similarly, in international relations it is easy to recognize the lack of political liberties in the Soviet Union, their domination of the nations in Eastern Europe, their obstructiveness in the United Nations, etc., but it is difficult for us to recognize similar defects in the United States: e. g., the disenfranchisement of most Negro voters in many

6

states, our domination of Latin America, our unfair treatment of the American Indian, our stubbornness in the UN in pretending that the representative from Taiwan is the representative of Mainland China. Since the mote-beam mechanism, obviously, works on both sides, there is a tendency for each side to view the other as peculiarly immoral and for the views to mirror one another.

What can be done to make the mote-beam mechanism ineffective? The proposals I have made to counteract the effects of the other type of perceptual distortions are all relevant here. In addition, I would suggest that the mote-beam mechanism breeds on a moral-evaluative approach to behavior, on a readiness to condemn defects rather than to understand the circumstances which produced them. Psychoanalytic work suggests that the capacity to understand rather than to condemn is largely determined by the individual's sense of self-esteem, by his ability to cope with the external problem confronting him, and by his sense of resoluteness in overcoming his own defects. By analogy, I would suggest that we in the United States will have less need to overlook our own shortcomings or to be fascinated with the defects of others to the extent that we have a thriving society which is resolutely overcoming its own problems of racial prejudice, economic stagnation, and lack of dedication to common public purposes.

7. Intense threat, fear, or conflict tends to impair perceptual and cognitive processes. When tension increases beyond an optimal, moderate level, it tends to impair perceptual and cognitive processes in several ways: it reduces the range of perceived alternatives; it reduces the time-perspective in such a way as to cause a focus on the immediate rather than the over-all consequences of the perceived alternatives; it polarizes thought so that percepts tend to take on a simplistic cast of being "black" or "white," "for" or "against," "good" or "evil"; it leads to stereotyped responses; it increases the susceptibility to fear - or hope - inciting rumors; it increases defensiveness; it increases the pressures to social conformity. In effect, excessive tension reduces the intellectual resources available for discovering to new ways of coping with a problem or new ideas for resolving a conflict.

There are several implications for international conflict. While it is apparent that some tension is necessary to help motivate attempts to resolve conflict, excessive tension may rigidify and stereotype the opposing positions. Moreover, since tension-tolerance is usually greater in thriving groups than in groups which are plagued by inner difficulties it is often easier to conduct reasonable and satisfactory negotiations when the parties in conflict are each internally secure. That is, it is often disadvantageous to fruitful negotiations to deal with a weak, insecure adversary. Thus, if my line of reasoning is correct it makes little sense for the United States to attempt to hinder the economic progress of the Soviet Union by trade and loan restrictions. Were the Soviet Union to experience serious economic difficulties and economic rebuff from the West, one might expect an even more rigid, hostile stance. I suggest that a lean and hungry China or Soviet Union

7

would be less amenable to reason than they would be if they were secure and well-fed.

While distortions in perception are very common for the reasons I have outlined above, it is also true that, in many instances, everyday experience provides a corrective. When reality is sufficiently compelling, and when the contact with reality occurs with sufficient frequency, they will be challenged and may yield. However, there are circumstances which tend to perpetuate and rigidify distortions. Let me briefly describe three major reasons for their perpetuation distortions:

1. A major psychological investment has been made in the distortion. As a consequence, the individual may anticipate that giving up the investment will require drastic personal reorganization which might result in personal instability, the loss of social face, or unknown dangers. Anyone who has done psychoanalytic therapy with neurotic patients knows that, no matter how costly and painful it is, a distorted but familiar mode of adjustment is hard to give up until the patient has sufficient self-confidence or confidence in his analyst to venture into unfamiliar terrain.

With regard to international relations, we have to consider that a disarmed world, a world without external tensions to justify internal political policies, a world without violence as a means of bringing about changes in the status quo would be an unfamiliar world; it would be a world in which some would feel that their vested interests might be destroyed. I am sure that many military men, scientists, legislators, industrialists, workers, and investors wish for but also fear a disarmed world because they anticipate that their skills, contacts, and knowledge will become obsolete, or because they expect to lose social status, or because they will fear financial loss. These fears have to be dealt with constructively or else they may produce defensive adherence to the views which justify a hostile, armed world. I suggest that we must carefully plan to anticipate the psychological difficulties in the transition to a peaceful, disarmed world. As a basic strategy to overcome some of these difficulties, I would recommend that we consider a policy of over-compensating those who might be adversely affected by the change: we want to change the nature of their psychological investment from an investment in military pursuits to one in peaceful pursuits.

2. Certain distorted perceptions perpetuate themselves because they lead the individual to avoid contact or meaningful communication with the object or person being perceived. Newcomb[9] has described a process of autistic hostility in interpersonal relations in which a hostile impulse may give rise to barriers to communication behind which a persistent attitude is protected. Similarly, in international relations, hostile attitudes between the U.S. and Communist China produce barriers to communication which eliminate the possibility of a change in attitudes. Here, the best antidote would seem to be communication which followed rules of procedure which required each side to state the other's position to the other's satisfaction.

3. Merton, in his classic paper on The Self-fulfilling Prophecy,[10]

8

has pointed out that distortions are often perpetuated because they evoke new behavior which makes the originally false conception come true. The specious validity of the self-fulfilling prophecy perpetuates a reign of error. The prophet will cite the actual course of events as proof that he was right from the very beginning. The dynamics of the self-fulfilling prophecy help to explain individual pathology - e. g., the anxious student who, afraid he might fail, worries so much that he cannot study, with the consequence that he does fail. It also contributes to our understanding of social pathology - e. g., how prejudice and discrimination against the Negro keeps him in a position which seems to justify the prejudice and discrimination. So too in international relations. If the representatives of East and West believe that war is likely and either side attempts to increase its military security vis-à-vis the other, the other's response will justify the initial move. The dynamics of an arms race has the inherent quality of a "folie à deux, " wherein the self-fulfilling prophecies mutually reinforce one another.

## The Conflict Between East and West

In the preceding section, I have attempted to indicate some of the sources of misperception in international relations and some of the conditions which tend to perpetuate the distortions or make them come true. However, one may ask whether I am suggesting that all international conflict is based upon misperception? Certainly not. There can be no doubt that there are accurately perceived conflicts - e. g., the conflict over tariffs between the U. S. and the Common Market countries in Europe, the conflict over the status of Taiwan, the conflict over the status of Central Europe.

What about the conflict between "East" and "West"? Public statements of the leaders of the two blocs define the conflict as a confrontation of two mutually irreconcilable ideologies; and it is apparent that basic ideological differences do exist. On the other hand, it must be borne in mind that neither the United States nor the USSR closely resemble its ideological "ideal type. " Neither Karl Marx nor Adam Smith would recognize his offspring.

Let us examine the central notions of each ideology. The key phrase of the American ethos is "life, liberty, and the pursuit of happiness. " The American vision is of the lone, independent, self-reliant, enterprising man who has escaped from the restrains of an oppressive community so as to be free to pursue his individual destiny in an environment which offers ever-expanding opportunity to those who are the fittest. The starting point of the Communist ethos is the view that man is a social animal whose nature is determined by the way men are related to one another in their productive activities in any given community. The Communist vision is of men who are free to cooperate with one another toward common objectives because they jointly own the means of production and share the rewards of their collective labor.

There is no need to detail here how far short of its ideal each system is, nor need to describe the many similarities in values and in

9

practices which characterize these complex, modern industrialized societies. One might even suggest that many - but certainly not all - of the differences which strike the casual observer of these two societies are differences which are due to differences in affluence and in national character rather than differences caused by ideological dissimilarities. In fact, neither ideology is more than an emphasis, a partial view of the total picture. Each side looks at the elephant from a different vantage point and, of course, describes it as two different beasts. However, this much can be said about the beast - the relation of the individual to society, the relation between individual liberty and social justice - it is a complex animal that has different needs and different characteristics at different stages of its development and in different environments. It is a poorly understood beast and only careful, objective study from all vantage points will give us insight into its care and nurture. But it is already evident that the beast needs both of its sides to function effectively. It needs individuals who are free to make their personal views and needs known, people who are neither conforming automatons nor slavish followers and it also needs a community which enables men to recognize their interrelatedness and to cooperate with one another in producing the social conditions which foster the development of creative, responsible people.

I suggest that neither the Marxist ideology nor the American ideology is consistent enough nor operational enough to be proved or disproved by empirical test. Nor is either specific enough to be a guide to action in the day-to-day decisions which shape the course of history. What, then, is the function of these ideologies? Primarily, they function, as do most myth systems, to help foster identification with and loyalty to the on-going social system. [11] They serve this function partly because an ideology is typically expressed in terms of some widely-appealing but vaguely-defined set of values - e. g., "life, liberty, and the pursuit of happiness" - which because of their presumably inherent rightness assures the ideological adherent of his righteousness and of his ultimate victory. Ideologies usually arise in the course of a conflict and for an adherent, an ideology not only defines who will win but also it defines who will lose: it delineates an enemy.

An external enemy or devil serves useful functions to those in power. It serves as a convenient excuse for internal difficulties and setbacks. It inhibits political criticism and social change by enabling those in power to identify the critics of the established order with the external devil. It promotes internal unity by rallying the group against external threat and, finally, it provides a rationale and justification for the segments of the society whose prestige, skills, financial interests, and institutional existence are based upon the belief that there is a devil. What would the demonologists do without a devil? It seems clear that the external devil of "exploiting capitalists" and "Wall Street imperialism" has served all of the above purposes for the Soviet Union, Castro's Cuba, and Communist China. In a similar way Communism has served as the devil for us.

I have stressed the fact that ideologies are vague. Vagueness permits diverse aspirations and changing practices to be accommodated

10

under the same ideological umbrella.  There are two important implications to be drawn.  First, it is useless to try to refute an ideology.
Moreover, since an ideology often serves important integrative functions, the attempt to refute it is likely to elicit defensiveness and hostility.  Like old soldiers, ideologies never die, they are best left to
fade away.  Second, the vagueness of ideologies permit redefinitions
of who is "friend" or "foe. "  There is ample room in the myth systems
of both the United States and the Soviet Union (or China) to find a basis
of amicable relations.

The conflict of the Cold War intensified our perception of ideological differences between "East" and "West. "  Now, however, as
internal conflicts within both "East" and "West" emerge (the Sino-Soviet
disputes and the Franco-American disagreements are only the more obvious cases) - we have an opportunity to revise our images of the nature
of the so-called "struggle between Communism and freedom. "  We have
more basis for recognizing that the ideological dispute is only the manifest rationalization of other less noble motives on both sides.  As
Freud pointed out the manifest life of the mind - what men know or pre-
tend to know and say about the motives of their behavior - is often
merely a socially acceptable rationalization of their unrecognized or
latent motives.  I suggest that the intensity of the ideological struggle
has primarily reflected an anachronistic power struggle between nations that have defined their prestige and security in terms of world
leadership.  It is much easier for Communists to rationalize an attempt
to subvert and overthrow a relatively progressive government in Vene-
zuela by thinking of it and calling it a tool of American imperialism
than to admit a crude attempt to weaken American power.  Similarly,
it is much easier for the United States to rationalize its support for
corrupt, dictatorial governments in Taiwan, South Korea, and South
Vietnam in terms of the defense of freedom than to consider it an attempt to maintain our power in Asia.

Traditionally, the quest for world power has been closely bound
to strivings for national security, economic dominance, and international prestige or influence.  The quest for power has commonly taken
the form of the attempt to establish military supremacy over one's
major competitors.  It is recognized increasingly that the drive for
military dominance in the age of missiles and hydrogen bombs is dan-
gerously anachronistic.  So too, economic imperialism - Western or
Eastern style - no longer provides as much opportunity for economic
gain as does a concentration upon scientific research and development.
However, the quest for international prestige and influence is a reasonable one for all societies.

Fair Rules For Competition

How can the competition for prestige and influence be kept
peaceful?  I suggest that we must develop fair rules for competition
and a cooperative framework which will develop allegiance and adherence to these rules.  Let me turn to a discussion of some fair rules.
A contest is considered to be fair if the conditions and rules of

the contest are such that no contestant is systematically advantaged or disadvantaged in relation to other contestants, the contestants have equal rights and opportunities, and the contestants are in the same category - i.e., they are more or less matched in characteristics relevant to the contest's outcome. Thus, it is manifestly unfair if the rules are such that the international contest permits non-Communist nations to become converted to Communism or to join an alliance with the Soviet Union but do not permit Communist nations or allies to be converted to the American side. Similarly, rules which would outlaw the establishment of a Communist nation in the Western hemisphere but not give a parallel right to the Soviet Union and Communist China hardly would be fair. Rules which put smaller, weaker nations - e.g., Cuba or Hungary - in a one-to-one contest with larger, powerful nations are not likely to lead to outcomes that are viewed as legitimate by the smaller nations.

The major international arena for rivalry between the big powers today is the underdeveloped countries of Africa, Asia, and Latin America. The competition for these "prizes" is mixed with arms and military confrontations. The danger of continued armed sparring in such places as Cuba, South Vietnam, South Korea, Laos, etc. is that misjudgment or despair may lead to an escalation of the armed conflict. We have lived through several close calls; it is time to rely on more than nerve and luck to avert disaster. I suggest that we take the initiative to propose fair rules for the competition of the "votes" or "allegiances" of the unaligned countries. As Amitai Etzioni has pointed out a set of rules would include such principles as the following:[12]

1. No non-aligned country would be allowed to have military ties with other countries, particularly not with any of the major powers.

2. No foreign troops or foreign bases or foreign arms of any sort would be permitted to remain in or enter the non-aligned country. Foreign arms would be prohibited to rebels and to the governments of non-aligned countries.

3. A United Nations observer force consisting largely of personnel from non-aligned countries and equipped with the necessary scientific equipment and facilities (flashlights, infra-red instruments, helicopters, aerial photography, lie detectors, and the like) to check the borders, ports, airfields, roads, railroads, etc. would be deployed at the request of any of the major powers or by the Secretary-General of the United Nations after a majority vote in the General Assembly. Costs would be allocated so as to reduce the incentive to create repeated false alarms.

4. A United Nations research and development staff would be established to keep informed about the development of new observational techniques and equipment.

5. Violations of the arms embargo would - once they were certified as such by an appropriate U.N. Tribunal - set in motion a cease and desist order aimed at the sender of arms or troops and a disarm order aimed at the receiver. Obedience to these orders would be checked by the U.N. observer force. Lack of compliance with the

orders to desist and disarm would result in sanctions appropriate to the nature of the violation - e. g. , a trade and communications embargo, a blockade, the sending of armed forces into the non-aligned country.

Would such a policy for the permanent military neutralization of the non-aligned countries be acceptable? Shortly after Stalin's death, the Soviet Union began to foster non-alignment among third countries under the slogan of a "vast zone of peace. " Since 1954, Soviet economic aid has gone to more than twenty underdeveloped countries, all of which - with the exception of Cuba - have maintained their independence and their status of non-alignment. Similarly, since late in Eisenhower's administration, the United States has been willing to give aid to countries that have not taken our side in the Cold War - e. g. , Jugoslavia. The non-aligned countries themselves have shown more and more desire not to become members of one or another military bloc. The time seems propitious for the super-powers, while they still remain dominant powers, to help establish the rules for non-armed competition for prestige and influence.

Suppose some such rules could, in fact, be established, what effects might be expected? Clearly, the revolutionary ferment in Asia, Africa, and Latin America would not disappear. Nor would it be unlikely that Communist governments would take power in some countries. These rules would not have prevented Castro from overthrowing Batista in Cuba. However, I suggest that the critical issue is not whether the local Communists or their sympathizers can achieve power in a given country without external military aid but rather whether after achieving power, they remain in power because of foreign military aid and whether they become a base for military aid to Communists in other countries.

Let us look at the issue of communism and the underdeveloped countries more directly. I suggest that a Communist government in an underdeveloped country presents no threat to us so long as it remains militarily unaligned. Such a government may be a tragedy to its people but we would be fulfilling our moral responsibility if we were to develop and enforce rules that could prevent outside military aid from foreclosing the possibility that the people will overthrow a government that is obnoxious to them. A Communist government that stays in power with the acquiescence of its people may be distasteful to us, and we may not want to aid it to stay in power, particularly if it is a terroristic government. But we can hardly claim the right to obliterate it. We do not intervene against such right-wing terroristic governments as those in Haiti, Paraguay, and Nicaragua. (To the contrary, we have given these terroristic governments military aid because presumably they are anti-Communist: military aid which could only be used effectively against their own people. )

The underdeveloped countries face incredibly difficult problems. The "revolution of rising expectations" has created aspirations that can not be fulfilled in the foreseeable future without massive aid from the richer nations. Even with massive aid (aid that would have to be many times more than is now being given), it would be a long and slow process before most of the underdeveloped countries reach an economic, educational, and technological level that will put them in reach of the standards of living found in modern industralized nations.

The Soviet Union cannot afford to give massive economic aid to many underdeveloped Communist nations. They cannot support many Cubas. Although we can afford to give much more aid than the Soviet Union and, in fact, to give much more than we do, our own capacities are not limitless. Both of our capacities could be considerably enhanced, as would the capacities of the recipients of such aid, if we could agree to keep arms and armed forces outside of the reach of the underdeveloped areas of the world. Too much of the assistance going to underdeveloped countries is in the form of military aid and too much of the production of underdeveloped countries is being channeled into military expenditures.

How would the United States make out in a competition for the free "vote" of the underdeveloped countries of the world? Would we do better than the Soviet Union, better than Communist China, better than France? I do not know but if we cannot do well in a free competition, perhaps we might consider the possibility that there is something wrong with us and had better revise many of our conceptions and ways of relating to other nations. We start off with many advantages. We have unsurpassed, and even unused resources to draw upon - we can turn out more food and more material goods than any other nation. We have a democratic tradition and the reputation of being the land of opportunity. The names of Washington, Jefferson, Lincoln, Roosevelt, and Kennedy are revered almost universally.

We also start out with disadvantages. We have identified ourselves with the status quo, with governments that are unwilling to institute the economic and political reforms necessary to make them responsive to popular aspirations. Also, the populations of most of the underdeveloped countries are non-white, and unfortunately, we have not yet overcome the pervasive practices of racial discrimination and segregation in our country. We are making progress but the progress is slow: the racial tyranny in Mississippi and the Negro ghettos in New York have not yet begun to disappear. It seems evident that unless we can achieve much more rapid and substantial progress in eliminating racial barriers at home, these barriers will obstruct us abroad. It also seems apparent that if we are going to be effective in the underdeveloped countries our aid has to be directed toward those governments which are attempting to increase their national productivity and to improve the lot of their populations. Aid to governments that are ineffective or aid to tyrannical rulers will not help the position of the United States in the international competition for prestige and influence. Too often our aid has gone to just such countries. Wouldn't our position in Latin America be somewhat better than it is now if Trujillo's accomplices, Duvalier's thugs, Stroesner's henchmen, and Battista's militia had not been armed with guns supplied by us? Surely, the guns in the hands of the tyrants and their accomplices should be supplied by someone else, not us.

The proposal I have made for the military neutralization of the underdeveloped countries has many technical problems which I have

14

ignored - e. g. , the nature and composition of observer forces, the composition and functioning of the Tribunal, the kinds of sanctions which might produce effective compliance. I assume that the major technical problems center about the need to reduce the likelihood that the rules can be violated in such a way as to give any side an insuperable advantage. Without going into this issue in detail, I think it can be seen that any given violation is not likely to have catastrophic consequences for the military security of any of the superpowers. And even if an underdeveloped country is subverted or taken over as a result of a series of violations, this is hardly likely to be catastrophic. Moreover, in such a case, the violations are hardly likely to be undetected. Thus, violations become evident before they become a substantial threat to one's security.

In other words, an agreement on fair rules for competition does not require a great deal of trust. It may be feasible in the kind of world that exists today. If the proposal were in fact implemented, it seems reasonable to think that it could be followed by such steps as a military neutralization of Central Europe, which could then lead to a massive reduction of the armed forces of the superpowers, which might be followed by a reduction of the strategic capabilities of the superpowers to a level of "minimum deterrence." Beyond that point, which seems remote in time, it seems unreasonable to speculate. If we get to that point, the world conditions will have been altered radically in ways which are not now predictable.

Developing a Cooperative Framework

Acceptance of fair rules for competition means an abandonment of cut-throat competition. It implies a change in the conception of one's adversary: he becomes a contestant rather than purely an enemy. The conflict changes its character. The rules which limit the forms of conflict, bind the contestants together in terms of common interests. However, the common interest in the rules is not, by itself, likely to be adequate to resist the debilitating effects of the inevitable misunderstandings and disputes which are associated with any system of rules. The bind between the contestants must be strengthened by enhancing their community or cooperative interests.

How can this be done? The key to the development of cooperation can be stated very simply. It is the provision of repeated and varied opportunities for mutually beneficial interactions. In relation to the Soviet Union, we have done some of this. But obviously not enough. Let me quote from a recent issue of the Wall Street Journal.[13]

Russia is ready, able, and anxious to become a good customer of the West - especially the U. S. - and equally eager for a chance to sell Western buyers its own wares.

The Soviets say they're ready to buy about $350 million of chemical equipment a year from the West over the next seven years, plus large quantities of construction equipment, farm tools, and other machinery.

15

On the selling side, the Soviets offer to conclude "long-term contracts of 10 and 15 years" to supply U.S. firms with Russian iron ore, manganese, chromium and other raw materials. The idea is to still any U.S. fears that the Soviets, who are often accused of using trade as a political weapon, might suddenly stop selling a commodity once a Western firm had become dependent on it.

And there's little doubt of the strength of Russia's desire to strengthen the USSR economy through trade with the West. To help make up for crop failures, the Soviet Union already has arranged to buy nearly $1 billion worth of Western wheat. To speed growth of its economy, it is relying largely on a $46 billion, seven-year program of building up chemical and related industries. Authorities estimate that nearly $2 billion worth of chemical equipment may have to be purchased from Western Europe, Japan, and the U.S. if this Soviet chemical program is to achieve its goals.

But trade with Russia runs into powerful political opposition from many Americans who feel it helps to strengthen a potential enemy. At present, any U.S. firm wishing to sell goods to Russia must get a Government license to export them, and licenses are supposed to be denied to "strategic" goods. The government before the wheat sale interpreted this injunction strictly enough to keep U.S. exports to Russia in 1962 down to a piddling $15 million.

A U.S. company wishing to import goods from Russia is free in most cases to buy as much as it likes. But to bring the goods into the U.S. it will pay a tariff three to four times as high as the duty of goods imported from other lands, and U.S. firms selling goods imported from Communist countries have often run into consumer boycotts. Such pressures in 1962 held U.S. imports from the Soviet Union to an insignificant $16 million.

Our reluctance to trade with the Soviet Union and our unsuccessful attempts to get our allies to limit their trade with them, the C.I.A.'s strange economic report on the Soviet Union are all indicators of an underlying view which hampers the attempt to strengthen cooperative bonds: the view that anything which helps them hurts us. Clearly, it helps them if their control over their nuclear missiles is such as to prevent accidental firings. But does this harm us? Clearly, it helps them if their children have available the Sabin polio vaccine. But does this harm us?

George F. Kennan has recently pointed out: "It is not too much to say that the entire /Communist7 bloc is caught today in a great crisis of indecision over the basic question of the proper attitude of a Communist country toward non-Communist ones. The question is whether to think of the world in terms of an irreconcilable and deadly struggle bound to end in the relatively near future with the total destruction of one or both, or to recognize that the world socialist cause can be advanced by more complicated, more gradual, less dramatic and less

immediate forms, not necessitating any effort to destroy all that is not
Communist within our time, and even permitting, in the meanwhile
reasonably extensive and profitable and durable relations with individual
non-Communist countries."[14]

None of us will fail to note that a parallel question tortures public opinion and governments in the West. There can be little doubt that
our answer to the question of whether Communist and non-Communist
countries can exist together peacefully will be an important influence
in determining how the Communists answer it. If we continue to maintain the quixotic notion that the Communist governments of Eastern
Europe, Cuba, China, and for that matter, the Soviet Union are likely
to disappear in some violent internal convulsion, will we influence
them to choose the less belligerent answer? Or will they be better influenced by a policy which accepts the reality of the Communist governments and adopts the view that we are willing to participate in any and
all forms of mutually beneficial interactions including normal diplomatic contacts, cultural and scientific exchanges, trade, and so forth.
Which policy provides a more promising prospect of a relaxation of the
severity of the Communist regimes and a weakening of the barriers
that separate their people from contact with the outside world? Which
policy is more likely to promote the growing individualism and diversity among the Communist nations? The answers are obvious. Yet so
many seem frightened by the idea of cooperation with the Communists;
the very phrase sounds subversive.

For many, appeasement and cooperation are equated. They
seem to feel that the only credible stance toward someone who might
have hostile intentions is a self-righteous, belligerent counter-hostility.
There is, of course, an alternative stance: one of firmness and friend-
liness. It is possible to communicate both a firm, unwavering resolve
not to allow oneself to be abused, intimidated, or defenseless and a
willingness to get along peacefully and to cooperate to mutual benefit.
In other words, willingness to cooperate does not imply willingness to
be abused.

"Firmness" in contrast to "belligerence" is not provocative and,
thus, while aborting the development of vicious spirals does not abort
the development of cooperation. It is, of course, difficult to resist the
temptation to respond with belligerence to the belligerent provocations
of some of the Communist nations. It requires a good deal of self-
confidence to feel that one does not have to demonstrate that one is
"man enough" to be tough nor that one isn't "chicken." If it just this
kind of firm, non-belligerent, self-confident, friendly attitude which
appears to be most effective in reforming aggressive delinquents.

Can we adopt such an attitude? Our defensiveness is rather
high, suggesting that we don't feel confident of ourselves. Our defensiveness comes from two sources. First, we have too high a level of
aspiration. Throughout most of our history, we have been in the
uniquely fortunate position of having pretty much our own way in foreign
affairs. Initially, this was due to our powerful isolated position in the
Americas and since World War II we have been the leading world power.
We face a loss of status. It seems evident that we cannot remain in the

17

unique status we have become used to. We can no longer be isolated from the physical danger of a major war nor can we remain the uniquely, powerful nation. We have to adjust our aspirations to the changing realities or suffer a constant frustration. A second root of our national defensiveness is a lack of confidence in our ability to maintain ourselves as a thriving, attractive society that can cope effectively with its own internal problems. The fact is that we have not been coping well with economic growth, unemployment, civil rights, the education of our children, the rebuilding of our cities, the care of our aged.

. . . . . . . I have now come full circle. Conflict is more likely to take the form of lively controversy rather than deadly quarrel when the disputants respect themselves as well as the other. The process of reforming another, of inducing an opponent to adhere to fair rules of competition, often requires self-reform. "Be not angry that you cannot make others as you wish them to be, since you cannot make yourself as you wish to be." Thomas à Kempis. "The heart of the wise teacheth his mouth, and addeth learning to his lips."

## Footnotes

1. P. Kecskemeti, Strategic Surrender, p. 209, Stanford University Press, 1958.
2. R. Fisher, ed., International Conflict and Behavioral Science, p. 7, Basic Books, 1964.
3. M. Deutsch, "The interpretation of praise and criticism as a function of their social context." Journal of Abnormal and Social Psychology, 1961, 62, 391-400.
4. U. Bronfenbrenner, "The mirror-image in Soviet American relations." Journal of Social Issues, 1961, 17, No. 3, 45-56.
5. S. Oskamp, "Attitudes toward U.S. and Russian actions: a double standard." Paper presented at the 1964 meetings of the California State Psychological Association.
6. S. E. Asch, "Studies of independence and conformity: I A minority of one against a unanimous majority." Psychol. Monog., 1956, 70, #416.
7. Much of this research is summarized in various articles in D. Katz, ed., "Attitude Change." Public Opinion Quarterly, 1960, 24, 163-365.
8. G. Ichheiser, "Misunderstandings in human relations." American Journal of Sociology, 1040, 55, (part 2), 1-70.
9. T. M. Newcomb, "Autistic hostility and social reality." Human Relations, 1947, 1, 69-86.
10. R. K. Merton, "The self-fulfilling prophecy" in his book, Social Theory and Social Structure, rev. ed., 1957, Free Press.
11. H. Wheeler, "Myth systems in American-Soviet Relations," Journal of Conflict Resolution, 1960, IV, 179-184.
12. A. Etzioni in Winning Without War, 1964, Doubleday, has devel-

oped these ideas at some length. My presentation is indebted to Etzioni's but differs in some of its details.

13. Monday, January 27, 1964.
14. George F. Kennan as quoted in <u>Current</u>, February, 1964, p. 13-14.

# ALLOWING FOR SOVIET PERCEPTIONS AND MOTIVES

Urie Bronfenbrenner
Cornell University

". . . since wars begin in the minds of men, it is in the minds of men that the defences of peace must be constructed. " So reads the preamble to the Charter for UNESCO to which both the United States and the Soviet Union are signatories. This statement implies that the successful prevention of war must take into account the mental processes going on in those societies that are most likely to become embroiled in another world conflict. In this perspective, it is a sobering fact indeed that among the millions being spent today for research on national security, almost nothing is being expended on systematic studies of what goes on in the minds of the Russians, their perceptions, fears, yearnings, and modes of thought.

Under such circumstances, even a crude assessment, limited by imperfect data and methods, can serve a useful purpose, if only to call attention to the kinds of results that might be obtained and the importance of their implications. Such are the nature and aim of the present paper. It draws on field observations, made in the course of two recent visits to the U. S. S. R. , in order to shed some light, however dim, on the Soviet image of American acts and intentions and on the motives and modes of thought which are most influential in producing that image. Such perceptions and predispositions are of the utmost importance. What influences Soviet policy toward war or peace is not our acts and intentions as we know them to be but as they appear in Soviet eyes.

## I.  Method

Before turning to substantive matters, a few words are in order about the technique employed for obtaining the data. On the surface, the procedure seems hardly worthy of being dignified as a "method" since it consisted simply of conversations with Soviet citizens. Nevertheless, the conversations did involve some special features which distinguish them from the typical discussions engaged in by Westerners in the U. S. S. R.  These features differed somewhat in each of two visits I have made during the past two years.

Open-ended Conversations. During the first visit, which occurred in May and June of 1960, the following practices were followed:
1.  Travelling alone without a guide.
2.  Wherever possible, departing from the Intourist trek; for example, eating in public restaurants instead of the large

Reprinted from International Conflict and Behavioral Science; The Craigville Papers, ed. R. Fisher, New York, Basic Books, 1964, by permission of the author and the publisher.

hotels, going about on foot or using public transportation, going to parks, places of recreation and other locales frequented by the general public, etc.

3. Taking the initiative in striking up conversations rather than waiting for others to do so.

4. In so far as possible, picking persons to talk with at random basis (e. g. , before going into an eating place, deciding in advance to sit at the third table on the right with whoever should be there).

5. Beginning with open-minded conversational leads rather than with pointed questions or positions.

6. Presenting self in the role of interpreter between East and West rather than as a militant proponent of the American view or as a Soviet sympathizer.

7. Not taking notes in the presence of the informant.

8. Keeping a record of informant's age, occupation, ethnicity, etc. , for subsequent analysis.

9. Using feedback to verify own perceptions (i. e. , asking my Soviet companion to listen to a restatement of his views and correct any omissions or distortions).

## A Pseudo-Experiment

During the second visit, which took place in November and December of 1961, the open-ended conversations were supplemented by procedures intended to maximize, in so far as possible, conditions favorable to communication. The procedures worked out following the first visit, jointly with a group of social science colleagues at Cornell,[1] are derived primarily from recent theory and research on social perception and communication. The underlying principle can be stated succinctly as follows: effective communication is most likely to occur if carried out in a context in which there has been prior recognition and, where possible, acceptance of some values cherished by the other party. Concrete examples of how this principle might be applied to improve our communications with the Russians (without compromising our own values) are provided in the report cited above.

Although originally developed for the Soviet case, the approach is presumed to have general validity. Accordingly, we undertook to pretest it first in the reverse direction: that is, in communicating with Americans about the Soviet Union. One of the specific techniques employed in this connection was the presentation of extended excerpts from the conversations collected during my earlier visit. Since these conversations typically involved a dialogue between an American and a Russian, the dissonant Soviet view was systematically balanced and offset by statements of the American position.[2]

I have described the above technique because it was used exactly in reverse during my second visit to the Soviet Union; in other words, I presented to the Russians excerpts from my conversations with Americans in which I had attempted to communicate the Soviet view, and my fellow countrymen had of course responded with statements of our own position and counter-argument. Actually, the sets of conversations used in the two countries were strikingly comparable, since, as has been documented elsewhere, [3] Soviet and American perceptions of each other are in many respects mirror images.

Use of similar materials in the two cultural settings made it possible to compare Soviet and American responses to analogous stimuli and to gauge the extent to which each group can be made to understand and accept dissonant information about the other. The results of this pseudo-experiment were instructive. There were clear similarities in the reactions of Russians and Americans, but even more striking differences. Although effective communication was achieved to some degree in both settings, Americans were more easily enabled to see the world through Soviet eyes than the reverse. In particular, certain approaches which worked very well with Americans (such as the presentation of factual evidence) were far less persuasive with Soviet citizens. Other techniques such as appeal to ideals or emotions, were more effective with Russians than with us. As a result, it became necessary to modify the approach to fit the special sensitivities and values of Soviet society.

## The Sample

To speak briefly about the nature of the sample over the course of the two visits, extended conversations were conducted with approximately 100 Soviet citizens in different walks of life ranging from unskilled laborers, through clerks and technicians, to factory managers, scientists, and party workers at the city, oblast, and republic level. Despite the effort at randomization, the sample was of course biased; from the perspective of the total Soviet adult population, there was an over-representation of urban residents, scientists, students, and those most likely to have contact with the visitor from the West -- Intourist personnel, other travellers, speculators, and the disaffected.

## II. Soviet Perceptions of Western Intentions

The open-ended interviews and structured stimuli yielded a wide range of data about Soviet perceptions and motives affecting the Russians' image of the United States. We shall examine first certain generalized attitudes bearing most directly on the issue.

Russian Fears of Western Attack. Such fears were the most salient and recurring feature of the Soviet conversations. Several lines of evidence point to the conclusion that they represented no mere perfunctory parroting of a propaganda line, but were genuine, intense, and virtually universal. First, the signs of fear were evident not only in what people said but in the way they said it; that is, in physiological reactions, voice quality, deterioration of speech pattern of the type associated with high levels of anxiety, etc.

Second, the expectation of Western aggression was evident even among those relatively few Russians who expressed criticism of the regime. Using the most liberal criterion possible by placing in this

22

category every person who made so much as one critical comment, however mild, approximately 25% of the sample fell in this group. [4] Yet, without exception all of them expressed the fear that the United States, spurred on by West Germany, would soon attack the Soviet Union. [5] Ironically enough, this expectation was held even by the very few persons I met who could be called anti-communists. For example, there was the 22-year-old Georgian baker who had taken part in the Tbilisi rebellion and wanted me to meet with a group of his fellow-conspirators; they were collecting ammunition and small arms, he said, in preparation for the day when the Americans would fly over to liberate the U. S. S. R.

It is important to recognize that, incredible as it may seem to us, from the Soviet point of view the evidence for Western aggressiveness appears consistent, continuing, and overwhelming. To Russians it is as plain and incontrovertible as Soviet aggression and treachery are to us. The major elements in the pattern include Allied intervention in 1918-20, the subsequent hostility of the outside world toward Communist Russia, the failure of collective security in the thirties, the horrible fulfillment of Soviet fears of attack from the West represented by the German invasion, the establishment of NATO, encirclement by Western bases, the rearmament of West Germany, and finally what are seen as recent signs of our renewed aggressive intent: the U2 incident, the Cuban affair, the arms build-up under the Kennedy Administration, the Supreme Court's decision against the American Communist Party (which was disillusioning and apparently quite disturbing to many Soviet citizens), public statements by leading American scientists (Teller, Libby, Kahn), Congressmen (Senators Goldwater and Dodd were mentioned specifically), and by John Birchers (the fact that they are permitted to speak is interpreted by the Russians as evidence of tacit Government support), war-like pronouncements in the press (e. g., articles from the Army and Navy Journal and Time's map showing arrows from Polaris to Moscow, Leningrad, and other large Soviet population centers), and of course, most recently our emphasis on inspection. For the Russians an intent on our part to carry out espionage seems obvious and inevitable. As a Deputy to the First Secretary of an oblast in the virgin lands explained it: "First you tried to fool us with your 'open skies' policy. When we wouldn't be taken in, you did your spying anyway with U2. Now that we've put an end to that, you need a new entry. So you try to trick us again the way the Germans did before World War II. They too deceived us into agreements so that they could wander about our country, spy out our defenses, and prepare their attack. "

The Threat of West Germany. The last remark illustrates the saliency of West Germany in Soviet fears. It is here that Soviet perceptions depart furthest from objective reality. The belief that West Germany is dominated by Nazi elements and, in turn, controls Western policy is widespread. There is the conviction that Americans are deliberately encouraging the resurgence of German militarism and are using West Germany as a base for anti-Soviet activities of espionage and subversion (e. g., Radio Liberty headquarters are in Munich).

23

The "Incredibility" of Deterrence. Perhaps the most disturbing aspect of the Russian image of the West as revealed in the conversations was the Soviet failure to "get the message" intended by the strategy of deterrence to which our present policy is committed. It is not that the Russians fail to understand that we will retaliate if attacked. This they readily, and spontaneously acknowledge. What is not getting across is the crucial part of the message: that we would never attack without provocation. When I tried to explain to Soviet citizens our purpose in shifting to "hard" and mobile missiles located away from centers of population, there were two common reactions. The first and less intense was to see the strategy as a ruse. "It is all part of a trick to get us off our guard while you secretly prepare for attack; besides, you don't really mean it because if you did, you wouldn't be doing all those other things." And once again the speaker would inundate me with talk of U2, Kennedy's arms build-up, and militant statements by leading figures in America and West Germany.

The second reaction to my explanations was both more common and more violent: "How can you even think this way! It is monstrous and inhuman to be so cold and calculating. You Americans just do not understand the horror, death, and destruction of modern war on your own soil. To talk of such a strategy as a way to peace is sheer madness." In short, it is not that our strategy of deterrence was non-credible; it was simple incredible.

A similar response of incredulity and reluctance even to discuss the subject was elicited when I sought to explain to more sophisticated Russians, such as scientists or members of peace study groups, the kind of research that was being done in the United States on arms control and related problems (e. g. , game theory, simulation techniques, probability sampling for zonal inspection, etc.). The reaction was almost one of shock. It was as if applying such technologies to peace were to profane holy ground.

III. Implications of Soviet Perceptions of the West

Before turning to still other Soviet orientations, it is important to examine possible limitations and implications of the material here offered on Russian attitudes towards the West.

The "Reality" of Perception. In presenting Soviet views of the outside world I am of course not implying that they are valid in the sense of being in accord with objective facts. Nevertheless, they are valid at another level. In the words of one of the pioneers of American social psychology, W. I. Thomas, "Situations defined as real are real in their consequences." In other words, the Russians are likely to act in accordance with their picture of the world, even though that picture may be grossly distorted. Because of this psychological fact, if we are to be realistic ourselves, we must treat Russian perceptions as if they were real, and consider their implications for Western strategy.

Communist Leadership vs. the Russian People. Granting that the rank and file of Soviet citizenry have irrational expectations of impending aggression from the West, do we really have any basis for concluding that similarly distorted perceptions and fears animate the Soviet leaders. After all, for the Russian people at large, the fears are fed by government-inspired propaganda. The leaders know this and, in addition, have other sources of information, including first hand experience with Westerners both within and outside the U. S. S. R. Surely, their views are not so unrealistic as those of the general population.

The data available to me permit no definitive answer to this question. Neither Comrade Khrushchev nor any other member of the Central Committee turned up in my random sample. Nevertheless, some indirect evidence may be relevant.

First, studies of other modern societies typically show substantial continuity in the views of the outside world held by the leadership and the population at large. Moreover, investigations of Nazi Germany suggest that in a totalitarian state this relationship is enhanced by the tendency of the leaders to believe their own propaganda.

Second, most of the men who are today leaders of the Soviet state held positions of responsibility immediately prior to and during World War II and hence were exposed, perhaps even more than the average Russian to the full impact of the deceit, destruction, and death wrought by the aggressor from the West. Such an experience is more likely to increase rather than diminish susceptibility to irrational expectations of treachery and sudden attack.

Finally, although I met none of the Communist inner circle, some of my informants were not far removed from this group. On one occasion after listening to a lengthy exposition from a fellow passenger, I commented that I had heard many ordinary Russians speak along similar lines but wondered about the rulers of the country, high ranking members of the party; did they feel the same way? "Well," my companion replied, a smile playing on his lips, "after this hour's conversation you are in a position to judge for yourself." He then explained that he was a member of the Supreme Soviet in his own Republic and assured me that similar views are held by members of the Central Committee of the all-Union Communist Party.

On another occasion, last December, I struck up a conversation on a plane with a chap who was much disturbed by what he regarded as evidence of increasing war hysteria in the United States. He had been discussing these matters with a friend and fellow-journalist who shared many of his own fears. As a matter of fact, this friend was now on a visit to the United States and hoped to get an interview with our President in order to talk with him about the dangerous American developments. Perhaps I had heard of his friend, since he was quite well-known in the Soviet Union; his name: Adzhubei.

The Importance of Context. If the Soviet leaders do share with their people an irrational fear of Western treachery and attack, what implications does this have for American strategy on arms control and prevention of war?

To begin with, we must recognize that any Western proposals will take their meaning for the Russians from this larger perceptual context. So long as the context remains unchanged, the likelihood is that any specific proposal will be viewed in such a way as to confirm the established image of American insidiousness and aggressive intent.

It is important to recognize that the forces driving the Russians to such invidious interpretation are of the most powerful kind and derive not only from historical and political, but also from compelling psychological factors. Over the past ten years there has accumulated in the behavioral sciences a substantial body of research demonstrating that human beings exhibit an extremely strong tendency to maintain consistency in their perceptions, particularly when these perceptions are shared by their fellows. New events are apprehended in such a way as to be compatible with previous experience and expectation. The tendency is so powerful that facts which, on objective grounds, seem incapable of any but a contradictory interpretation are re-organized so as to maintain consistency.

Soviet citizens and their leaders are certainly as susceptible to this mechanism as any other group; indeed, as we shall show later, there are grounds for supposing that they may be especially vulnerable to such tendencies. In any event, with specific regard to American arms control proposals to date, the Russians have for several reasons found it very easy to perceive confirmation for their worst expectations. First, as we have already noted, prior experience seems to them unequivocal and compelling. Second, we give virtually no thought to the larger context of action by the United States and the West which may precede or accompany the presentation of the proposal. Third, we typically do little to "immunize" the proposal itself against invidious interpretations in line with Soviet expectations. And once the Russians see the meaning of our proposal in their terms (e. g., inspection equals espionage), it becomes part of the cumulating evidence confirming American treachery and aggressive intent.

The preceding considerations lead to an important operating principle: any concrete proposals we wish to make must be prepared for by prior and simultaneous actions in other spheres which enhance the likelihood that the particular proposal will be seen in a new and less threatening context. In addition, the proposal itself must, in so far as possible, be "immunized" against invidious interpretations.

The Problem of Seeing through Soviet Eyes. Paradoxically, if American strategists were to take the unlikely step of adopting the foregoing principle and seeking to apply it forthwith, the results would probably be ineffectual, if not disastrous. Soviet behavior is determined by Soviet perceptions, Soviet fears, and Soviet modes of thought. Any attempt to predict how the Russians would react which is based solely on considerations of strategy, deductive reasoning, and the assumption (usually unrecognized) that Soviet thought processes are similar to our own is doomed to miss the mark. Given our own necessarily limited perspective, we cannot arrive at an appreciation of the springs of Soviet action solely through the power of logical analysis, no matter how rigorous, or of creative imagination, no matter how ingenious. As the essential starting point for our estimates we need first to obtain and analyze data which can instruct us about the nature of Soviet perceptions, motives, and fears. Moreover, if the assumptio

of cultural continuity in attitudes has any validity whatsoever, in order
to have relevant information, we need not wait until we can install
wire-taps in the Kremlin or get Khrushchev on the psychoanalytic
couch.

As a case in point, let us consider how one might go about
studying possible Soviet reactions to American proposals on arms control. Here are two examples from the range of investigations which
could be carried out.

1. Analysis of published materials. Soviet reactions to
   American proposals for arms control appear periodically in
   Soviet newspapers and specialized journals. Such reactions
   include review of Western books and articles on the subject
   as well as Russian translations from these, in part or in
   full. Such materials need to be analyzed systematically not
   from the point of view of military or political strategy but
   for what they reveal of Soviet motives, needs, and tendencies to distorted perception. Particularly instructive in
   this connection is the choice of material presented, omissions or alterations in a translated text, etc. The technology for carrying out analyses of this kind already exists.

2. Interviews with Soviet citizens. Soviet attitudes may be
   assessed at still another level through systematic application of a procedure employed informally by the writer during a recent visit to the U.S.S.R. An inventory was prepared representing a range of proposals now current in
   Western thinking. In the course of conversation, Soviet
   citizens were asked to comment on which proposals were
   most constructive, which least so, and why. The responses
   were particularly instructive in identifying possible Soviet
   reactions that might not be anticipated by the Westerner
   (e.g., withdrawal from bases near Soviet borders was con-
   sistently preferred to demobilization of Atlas missiles or
   Polaris submarines; Western proposals in which the Soviet
   commitment was made explicit were adjudged less threatening than unilateral "tension-reducing" action by the West,
   which were regarded as devious and manipulative in intent).

Minimizing Associations with Nazi Germany. If it is correct
that Soviet views of the West become most distorted where associations
with Nazi treachery and invasion are aroused, it becomes important to
avoid any explicit or chance similarity to past Nazi practices. This,
in turn, requires that we become familiar with the nature of German
activities with regard to U.S.S.R. especially in the period of the Nazi-
Soviet pact and, of course, during the invasion itself. Such studies
should focus major attention on Russian sources, since it is these
which provide the basis for current Soviet attitudes.

What Follows from Fear? Implicit in the preceding recommen-
dations is the assumption that development of strong Soviet fears of the
West decreases the possibility of agreement on measures for arms control and, more generally, consistutes a danger to the security of the
United States. But there exists a contrary view. There are those who

maintain, for example, that it is precisely fear of the West which is needed to convince the Russians of the necessity of arms control; the more ominous the danger to them, the more likely they are to realize the necessity of coming to terms. Indeed, the strategy of deterrence, on which our whole policy is based, relies on fear as the inhibitory force to Soviet aggression. If we allay Soviet fears in the interests of increasing Soviet receptivity to proposals for arms control, we may at the same time be undermining the major barrier to Communist expansion.

This line of reasoning also rests on certain assumptions, and it is useful to make these explicit. First, there is the expectation that an American build-up of arms will lead the Russians to fear American military might. As we have seen, this expectation appears to be fully justified.

Second, there is the assumption that if we shift to hard and mobile missiles, move rocket sites away from cities, and explain what we are doing, the Russians will be convinced by such action that we would never attack unless provoked. Hence, the only thing they have to fear is their own aggressive initiative. But if we are correct in expecting some continuity between the perceptions of the Soviet people and their leaders, the evidence cited above raises some question about the validity of the preceding assumption, especially so long as a substantial portion of the other "messages" coming from the West to the Soviet Union communicate quite a different intent.

Third, there is the assumption that as the United States becomes objectively stronger than the Soviet Union, the latter will feel weaker, more vulnerable, and hence will become more tractable and less likely to initiate aggression.

Finally, implicit in the entire argument is the assumption that the Soviet Union will appraise its own situation rationally and will adopt the course of action indicated by logical analysis of the strategic considerations involved.

The last two assumptions go beyond Russia's image of the United States; they deal with the Soviet Union's conception of itself and with the manner in which Soviet society is likely to respond to situations of threat and conflict. We turn next to a consideration of these topics in the light of such evidence as is available from the Soviet conversations.

## IV. The Soviet Self-Image

Next to fear of the West, the most salient feature of the conversations was the Russians' preoccupation with their own national image. This preoccupation manifested itself in a number of ways: in expressions of Soviet righteousness in international affairs, invincibility, pride, and extreme sensitivity.

The Russians' View of Soviet Aggression. Perhaps the remarks of Soviet citizens most dissonant to Western ears are those relating to what we regard as flagrant examples of Communist aggression. With only a few exceptions, the Russians with whom I spoke viewed with what appeared to be genuine approval the actions taken by

their rulers in Czechoslovakia, Poland, Germany, Hungary, and elsewhere round the globe. Specifically, they saw their government as
having given deserved assistance to forces of progress and due warning
and rebuff to impending aggressive moves by the West. A case in point
was the reaction of Soviet citizens to Russian resumption of nuclear
testing, which had occurred only a few weeks before my last visit.
While acknowledging the dangers of escalation and fall-out, all the Russians with whom I spoke uniformly approved Khrushchev's decision as
one that had been forced by what they viewed as signs of increasing
American belligerence and preparation for a first strike.

The Conviction of Invincibility. Paradoxically, in the same
breath with statements of their fear of attack from the West and the
horrors of war, Russians would cock the head and speak defiantly of
ultimate victory. I remember two balladeers performing in a public
square. The first song was "Do the Russians Want War" (Ask my
mother, ask my wife.). Then, directly after, a melody in martial beat
ending with: "But if imperialists come in, look out! Our habit is to
win!" The audience shook their heads earnestly to the first song, and
nodded proudly to the second. I pressed one Soviet citizen for the basis
of such convictions. His reply, "We shall beat you not because we are
superior militarily, not because we have a sounder economy, but because we are stronger morally." Shades of Sir Galahad!

Soviet Pride and Sensitivity. Coupled with a sense of national
righteousness and invincibility was an inordinate pride in Soviet achievements in all spheres -- educational, economic, scientific, artistic,
and social. People were constantly pointing out not only to the foreigner
but to each other (especially to children) that this or that was first,
newest, largest, or best. At the same time, the sensitivity to criticism
was acute. Russians were quick to interpret casual words or actions
as slurs on the national honor. For example, to take photographs of
anything but the very ancient or the very new was to risk public censure;
an unfavorable comment about a building, play, or administrative procedure was interpreted as a reflection on the entire Soviet society.

What is most significant about these reactions was their irrational quality. In speaking of achievements, Soviet citizens -- including persons holding positions of considerable responsibility -- often
made statements about products and performances that were patently
untrue and denied inadequacies visible to the naked eye. Moreover, the
accompanying gestures, tone of voice, and physiological reactions were
of a kind which suggested that they were engaging not in calculated mis-
representation but in involuntary distortion born of inner tension. In
other words, at least at that moment, they believed what they were saying; they were deceiving themselves.

In the same measure that criticism evoked violent defense, denial, or counterattack, praise of one or another aspect of Soviet society
elicited equally disproportionate reactions of enthusiasm and personal
warmth. The hunger for praise and prestige was impressive. Of particular interest in this connection was the effect of praise on communication. Ideas which previously seemed not to be understandable were
now not only comprehended but even half-accepted.

In order to examine the implications of these national attitudes and reactions for American policy it is necessary first to set them in the larger context of the general pattern of response to conflict situations in Soviet society.

## V. Modes of Adaptation in Soviet Society

We have noted that in the sphere of international and national behavior, Soviet citizens tend to see the West as the source of all evil and their own nation as "the best of all possible worlds." Any defects in the latter are either denied or described as vestiges of capitalism (and now, of Stalinism). Thus vice and virtue are conveniently separated geographically and politically; all, of course, to the benefit of the Soviet image. It is a convenient, if unrealistic, way of dealing with the world.

Patterns of Response in Everyday Life. Curiously enough, during my visit, I first became aware of this mechanism not at the international but at the mundane level. In observing individual Russians confronted by everyday problems, mistakes, and personal differences, I noted repeatedly a ready resort to these same mechanisms of denial and displacement. A store clerk, unable to find her pad of receipts would immediately accuse her working companion, and, even when the object turned up on her own desk, would insist that the other had taken and surreptitiously replaced it. Or a person who had failed to show up for an appointment would accuse his companion of having failed to appear. In like manner, mistrust, self-righteousness, and sensitivity to criticism were manifest in many spheres besides the patriotic.

Reactions of this kind can of course be observed in any society. Moreover, one is more likely to notice them when traveling in a country that is seen as a potential enemy.

For this reason, the results of the pseudo-experiment described earlier are particularly important. The experiment, it will be recalled, required that in both cultures, analogous stimuli consisting of dissonant material be presented in what was intended to be an acceptable context. Unfortunately, since I was feeling my way, the procedures for eliciting and recording responses were not kept constant. But the differences in reaction in the two settings were sufficiently great to override these limitations. As already mentioned, it proved far easier to get an American to change his picture of the Soviet Union than the reverse. Although showing some capacity for change, Soviet citizens were much more likely than Americans to hang on to their stereotypes and defend them by denial and displacement.

It is of course true that in this pseudo-experiment the stimuli were always being presented by an American, who was recognized as such in both settings. During the past year, however, I had a recurrent opportunity of observing American reactions to statements made by Soviet students living in the United States. Although these statements were not made in as acceptable a topical context as mine had been, the American reactions to the communist source were very similar to those

30

observed in the pseudo-experiment.

In short, I am persuaded that a comparative study of modes of adaptation in American and Soviet society would reveal a stronger predilection in the latter for black-and-white thinking, moral self-righteousness, mistrust, displacing of blame to others, perceptual distortion, and denial of reality.

Individual vs. Group Psychology. One might conclude from the foregoing paragraph that I judge the Russians to be psychiatrically ill, that they are disturbed personalities as resistant to change as patients suffering from classical paranoia. This might well be the conclusion suggested by traditional psychology, for it used to be thought that if people distorted reality, it meant that they were sick, and their illness, if not hereditary, was the product of a unique personal history of trauma, especially in early childhood. There is no doubt that such early experience can lead to serious disturbance. In the past twenty years, however, there has been considerable research in social psychology which demonstrates that perfectly healthy persons, when placed in certain kinds of social situations, experience perceptions and exhibit behavior which are quite inappropriate when judged against objective standards. As an example, we may cite the effect first shown in a set of experiments by Solomon Asch and thereby known as the "Asch phenomenon."[6] In these experiments, the subject finds himself in a group of six or eight of his peers all of whom are asked to make comparative judgments of certain stimuli presented to them, for example, identifying the longer of two lines. At first the task seems simple enough; the subject hears others make their judgments and then makes his own. In the beginning he is usually in agreement, but then gradually he notices that more and more often his judgments differ from those of the rest of the group. Actually the experiment is rigged. All the other group members have been instructed to give false responses on a predetermined schedule. In any event, the effect on our subject is dramatic. At first he is puzzled, then upset. But soon he is reassured, for he begins to "see" the stimuli as they are described by his fellows.

Conditions Fostering Distortion and Denial. Experiments like these have demonstrated that the fear of social deviance can be a very powerful force in determining what one perceives or does not perceive; that is, it can lead both to distortion and denial. Other investigations have identified additional factors which contribute to such perceptual tendencies. These include the following conditions:

1. Exposure to pressure for achieving excessively high or unattainable standards of performance.
2. Situations in which deviation or failure implies moral culpability or weakness and entails public disapproval or ostracism.[7]
3. Situations in which criteria for objective comparison are minimal or absent.
4. Identification with a social group that is striving for upward mobility from a relatively inferior status.

It is noteworthy that all four of these conditions are met in

31

present-day Soviet society.

The Impact of Historical Experience. But in addition to these contemporary pressures, the Soviet people are constrained by psychological forces deriving from their national history which likewise predispose them to exaggerate their achievements and to deny internal defects. These forces have been discussed in greater detail elsewhere, [8] and may be summarized by the following quotation:

> The deprivation, oppression, suffering and unceasing labor that the Soviet people have had to bear over the last several decades could be endured only in the name of some almost superhuman goal. To question the effort or the accomplishment is to make this anguish all in vain. Hence the sensitivity, defensiveness and pride of Soviet leaders and citizens alike, especially when their aspirations and achievements are called into question.

The Dynamics of Distorted Perceptions. The preceding analysis leads to the conclusion that instances of Soviet distrust, double-dealing, and denial are motivated by much more than purely strategic considerations. They are not so much products of logical analysis and deliberate decision as expressions of deeply-internalized, powerful emotional needs that have become part of an enduring cultural pattern. It is these needs which underlie the distorted perceptions we have described as characteristic of Soviet society.

It is therefore a matter of some interest to inquire how such distorted perceptions are affected by and in turn affect objective events. What happens, for example, when such images are directly challenged by contradictory evidence? Or when they are given confirmation by events in the external world? Do either of these conditions serve to dissipate the distorted picture? If not, are there other forces that can be invoked to this end? Finally, under what circumstances do people act in accordance with their distorted perceptions, and how, if at all, can such action be forestalled?

Unfortunately, the behavioral sciences are as yet far from definitive answers to such questions. Some knowledge does exist, however, which though crude and tentative, may yet foreshadow the general outlines of future research results. For example, there is evidence to suggest that when distorted perceptions are directly challenged, instead of being dispelled they are defended even more forcefully by more radical means. There are also indications that a similar reaction occurs when irrational fears and expectations are confirmed by reality. In short, any objective event which increases internal anxiety enhances resort to perceptual defenses. It also increases the likelihood of tension release through overt behavior responsive to the perceived threat. Conversely, the likelihood of distorted perceptions and irrational behavior is reduced as sources of anxiety and threat are removed. For example, in the Asch experiment the presence of a single confederate who reports objectively almost eliminates the experimental effect; the subject is again able to see what is actually there.

In the light of this analysis of the dynamics of perceptual distortion and defense, we are now in a position to return to a consideration of the major focus of this inquiry.

## VI.  Some Implications of Soviet Psychology for American Policy

Some Ominous Possibilities.  If the preceding analysis of modes of adaptation characteristic of Soviet society is valid, it raises serious questions about the consequences of any American strategy which seeks to communicate our intentions primarily through the building up and selective deployment of weapons and which assumes that Soviet action will be determined through a process of rational weighing and decision among possible outcomes.  On the contrary, the evidence suggests that a strategy of this kind is likely to enhance irrational fears, thereby increasing tendencies to distortion, distrust, denial, and the need to attack an external scapegoat.  Particularly with respect to the Soviet Union, if these pressures from without coincide with internal crises, such as agricultural failures or economic shortages, we risk the possibility that Stalinist elements within the Communist party will once more gain the upper hand and the Soviet Union will return to an era of regimentation and paranoid nationalism.

Such a conclusion should not be taken to imply the view that militant communism is merely a product of psychological forces.  There can be no doubt, for example, that Marxist ideology, with its injunction to further the inevitable triumph of communism, the fervent belief in its own perfection, and the frightening vision of implacable capitalist hostility, strongly reinforces and in turn is strongly reinforced by the psychological processes we have been describing.  But our concern is to identify the most alterable of the conditions which, on the one hand, are likely to magnify the total complex of forces to dangerous proportions or, on the other, to reduce its intensity and strengthen such potentiality for liberalization as may exist in contemporary Soviet society.

With this two-fold objective in view, it is useful also to examine the implications of our analysis within the more restricted area of measures for arms control.  Here our line of reasoning suggests that any procedures which have the consequence of confronting the Russians with their own deficiencies and self-delusions are likely to arouse the strongest resistance.  Indeed, one might hazard the prediction that even if the Russian leaders were to agree in good faith to the kind of inspection procedures we have been insisting upon, they would ultimately be forced to renege; otherwise they might not be able to stay in power.

In a still broader perspective, our analysis would seem to justify only the greatest pessimism regarding any kind of arms control agreement with the U.S.S.R., for, in effect, it asserts that the Russians cannot be trusted even when they themselves are earnestly trying to be sincere.

A Counteractive Approach.  Certainly the outlook is not sanguine, at least in the short run, but neither is it as hopeless as might appear.  The very psychological characteristics which make the

Russians susceptible to irrational fears, distortions, and displacements also present opportunities for encouraging their movement in other directions. For example, we have already referred to the Soviet craving for recognition and prestige and the disporportionate positive reaction which response to this craving elicits. Needs of this kind could be responded to in order to counterweigh other, more obstructive tendencies, such as the Soviet penchant for secrecy.

It is difficult to give actual examples, primarily because we have so seldom availed ourselves of such opportunities. One instance, however, does come to mind: our granting of an interview with the President to Mr. Adzhubei with the understanding that the text of the interview would be published in the Soviet press. I had the opportunity of observing that the Russians kept their part of the bargain even in such far-away republics as Kazakhstan. For the first time the views of an American President were presented in full to the Soviet people.

This single example suggests how much might be accomplished if we took occasion more frequently to acknowledge genuine accomplishments and achieved status in the Soviet world.

Incentives to Positive Response in Soviet Society. But recognition of achievement and acknowledgment of prestige are but two of many modes of behavior by a Westerner that evoke in Russian citizens a positive response all out of proportion to the stimulus. In the Soviet conversations, topics which had a similar effect included discussions of Soviet suffering in World War II, of education, science, poetry, children, and -- especially -- peace. In fact, a good guide to Soviet psychological hungers is what one reads about in their own newspapers. For the reasons we have already indicated, the Russians are the best consumers and the most ready victims of their own propaganda. [9]

There is one important exception to the preceding generalization. Paradoxically, the Russians are remarkably responsive to expressions of American idealism. Unfortunately, the key concept here is not the one we have been using. For ideological reasons, the word freedom has for Soviet citizens a connotation of irresponsibility and license. The traditional American value that has unambivalent appeal is human dignity. To the Russian, this quality is perhaps best symbolized in the person of Abraham Lincoln, who, ironically enough, is something of a national hero in the U.S.S.R. (Three years ago there was a sesquicentennial celebration of Lincoln's birth, involving national ceremonies, special editions of his writings, and a new biography prepared for general use in the schools.) A reaffirmation, in our dealings with the Soviet Union, of our commitment to Lincolnian ideals, might contribute in some measure to evoking a less antagonistic response.

Finally, at the most general level, perhaps the greatest contrast suggested by the results of the pseudo-experiment was the differential power in the two cultures of exposure to facts vs. feelings. In general, American respondents were influenced most by being presented with the objective evidence about Soviet society; any feelings I may have had on the subject, including antagonistic ones, were best kept in the background. Quite the opposite with the Russians; if I wanted to convey something of the American outlook, I had to rely on affect to carry the message. Communication was most successful when one spoke in the name of ideals and feelings rather than invoking evidence and logic. The lofty principle had to come first; only then could facts be introduced, and even so, preferably as inevitable deductive necessities, rather than as empirically independent observations.[10]

In short, the Russians take attitudes and emotions much more seriously than we. It is this which explains their over-reaction to American demagoguery as reflected in our public media. At the same time, we could turn this sensitivity to our own account in our dealings with the Russians by drawing more heavily on our own rich idealistic traditions.

The Persuasive Effect of Modest Commitment. A recognition of Soviet fears and motives does not exhaust the possible contributions of a psychological approach to American policy. For example, it is a common observation, confirmed by research, that people ordinarily believe themselves safe in making small concessions, since they can always stop short of the next step if they so desire. Actually, psychological studies on persuasion indicate that commitment to one step has the effect of changing attitudes toward the next. This means that it may be to our advantage to involve the Russians in agreements which we do not regard as fully adequate (provided, of course, that such agreements do not seriously endanger our own security). Once committed, the Russians may be more likely to take what we regard as a truly consequential step.

The Place of a Psychological Approach. In urging adoption of a psychological perspective in considerations of American policy, I am not arguing for the elimination of other more traditional considerations. Were American decisions to be guided substantially by psychological concerns to the neglect of military, political, economic, and other factors, the outcome would be tragic indeed. But it is the major thesis of this paper that the converse of the foregoing proposition is equally valid. To base our arms control and disarmament policy primarily on considerations of strategy and rational analysis is to court disaster just as surely. It is true that we know less of psychological realities than of military and political ones. The assessments offered above regarding Soviet perceptions and motives and their strategic implications are at best hypotheses. But the means for checking these hypotheses, and arriving at better ones, are at hand. The required research is admittedly difficult but do-able. And until our information becomes more firm, we can, at the least, give serious consideration to the dangers and possibilities suggested by existing theory and knowledge. For the most likely and most disastrous error the United States can make is to misjudge Communist perceptions and predispositions to action.

Footnotes

1.   "A New Approach for Communicating with the Russians." Report prepared by a working group of Cornell faculty members.

35

Available from the Cornell Center for International Studies.
2.  For other, quite different applications of the general principle in
    the American context see the following:
    Bronfenbrenner, U., "Secrecy: A Basic Tenet of the Soviets."
    N. Y. Times Magazine, April 22, 1962.
    _____, "Possible Effects of a Large-Scale American
    Shelter Program on the Soviet Union and Other Nations."
    Report prepared for submission to the Armed Services Com-
    mittee of the House of Representatives, May 1962.
3.  Bronfenbrenner, U., "The Mirror Image in Soviet-American Rela-
    tions." Journal of Social Issues (1961), 17, 45-56.
4.  For some concrete examples see Bronfenbrenner, U., "The Mir-
    ror Image in Soviet-American Relations," Op. Cit. This report
    also discusses other methodological problems bearing on the
    validity of the material obtained.
5.  It is of interest to note that, among these, a disproportionate num-
    ber were members of minority groups (Jews, Georgians,
    Estonians, and Armenians), were either under 25 or over 50
    years of age, and had taken the initiative in seeking me out.
    The last observation raises some question about the validity of
    Soviet disaffection based on conversations with Soviet citizens
    who have gone out of their way to talk with Western observers.
    When asked about their bases for such beliefs, Soviet citizens
    frequently cited, in addition to their own press and radio, Ameri-
    can broadcasts to the U. S. S. R. Especially salient in this regard
    were quotations from speeches by American military figures and
    Congressmen.
6.  Asch, S. E., "Studies of Dependence and Conformity: I. A Minority
    of One against a Unanimous Majority," Psychological Mono-
    graphs, 1956, 70 (9), 70 pp.
7.  Especially significant in this connection are the methods of child
    rearing being employed in Soviet nurseries, boarding schools,
    and youth groups. See Bronfenbrenner, U., "Soviet Methods
    of Character Education: Some Implications for Research."
    American Psychologist, August 1962, 17, 8, 550-564.
8.  Bronfenbrenner, U., "Secrecy: A Basic Tenet of the Soviets."
    Op. Cit. This article also points to bases in Communist ideol-
    ogy which further perceptual distortion; e. g., Lenin's thesis
    that subjective experience is a direct reflection of objective
    reality.
9.  Such a consideration argues for the importance of conducting sys-
    tematic studies of Soviet domestic propaganda as a guide to
    psychological needs in contemporary Russian society.
10. This phenomenon reflects the influence of dialectic materialism on
    thought processes in Soviet society. One arrives at reality --
    especially social political reality -- by deduction from Marxian
    doctrine.

# SIMULATION RESEARCH IN INTERNATIONAL DECISION-MAKING[1]

Lawrence N. Solomon[2]

## Behavioral Research for Peace

Though one of mankind's most enduring dreams is that of a "peaceful world, " rarely has the concept of peace been seriously examined or explicated, nor has the empirical meaning of a "peaceful world" been fully explored. Peace is still, after many millenia, a tantalizing mirage. Man's hard-won but as yet limited understanding of himself has not brought that self-acceptance which would enable him to see man as truly "the measure of all things. " Yet this fundamental self-acceptance is essential if we are to develop a theory of peace which is soundly based on a biosocial human ethic. As John W. Burton writes:

> A theory of peace opens up many new fields of inquiry. The important aspects of the study of international relations are not international organization, deterrents, resource distribution, balance of power, and the many other matters which frequently are included in conventional studies of the subject. The important ones in the nuclear era are aspects not as yet investigated; the nature of the responses, the processes of adjustment, and behaviorist studies not previously thought to be of concern to the student of international relations. (Burton, 1962, p. 189)

Since it is in the minds of men that wars begin -- and there that the defenses of peace must be built -- scientific research on war and peace should aim, in part, at furthering our understanding of those psychological processes and behaviors upon which international relations are predicated. One of the most promising approaches to a behavioristic investigation of such phenomena is to be found in the simulation studies of international decision-making. Within the constraints of a simulated international system, all types of persons can be called upon to respond, as decision-makers, to a variety of experimental conditions modeled on "real world" situations. This enables the observed

---

[1] The presentation of this paper at the International Congress of Applied Psychology in Ljubljana, Yugoslavia, August 7, 1964, was enabled by support from Northwestern University's International Relations Program under Office of Naval Research Contract Nonr-1228 (22), when the author was Executive Secretary of the American Psychological Association's Committee on Psychology in National and International Affairs.

[2] Currently, Research Associate, Western Behavioral Sciences Institute, La Jolla, California.

interrelations between the sub-units of the international system (i. e., nations, decision-makers, and economic, military, and political variables) as well as the effects of personality variables, to be studied both for research and for teaching purposes.

This paper describes a simulation technique developed by Harold Guetzkow and his associates at Northwestern University, called the Inter-Nation Simulation (INS), and briefly reviews a selection of recent INS studies.

## An Overview of the Inter-Nation Simulation Model

The INS is "an operating representation in reduced and/or simplified form, of relations among social units by means of symbolic and/ or replicate component parts." (Guetzkow, 1962, p. 84). A miniature world of fictitious nations is created by requesting individuals to take the role of decision-makers for each of a number of "nations, " to attempt to maintain themselves in office through the successful fulfillment of their decision-making obligations, and to play out the course of events which develop within the system according to the dictates imposed both by their own philosophies of international relations, and by the constraints of the simulated international system.

Usually, each "nation" is manned by four decision-makers: the Central Decision-Maker (the CDM), analogous to a Chief-of-State; the External Decision-Maker (the EDM), analogous to a Minister of Foreign Affairs; the Decision-Maker for Force (the DMF), analogous to a Minister of Defense, and an Aspiring Decision-Maker (the CDM$_a$), analogous to the leader of the major opposition.

The decision-makers are given a brief historical orientation as to the nature of the "world" within which they are to operate; they are provided with an array of resources and growth-rates which define the economic and military characteristics of their own particular nation; and they are informed as to the degree of domestic freedom in decision-making they are allowed by their "nation" (i. e., how responsive they must be to those who validate their decisions).

The allocation of resources provides the major decisional task for each "national" team, and produces military, economic, and political consequences in both domestic and international spheres. The way resources are allocated during each period of play, and the motives underlying these allocation-decisions, provide two major sources of data.

Each period of play represents a highly compressed segment of time; e. g., 70 minutes of play may represent a year of "real world" time. A "run" usually comprises 8 to 15 periods; and an INS project may encompass 10 to 15 "runs" in which a different set of teams is used for each run.

Figure 1 diagrams the interrelations among the many variables, programmed and unprogrammed, in the INS model. This Figure is taken from Wayman Crow's article on the use of the INS for the study of strategic doctrines (Crow, 1963); I shall therefore draw upon his exposition.

FIGURE 1

ALLOCATION OF RESOURCES AND CONSEQUENCES

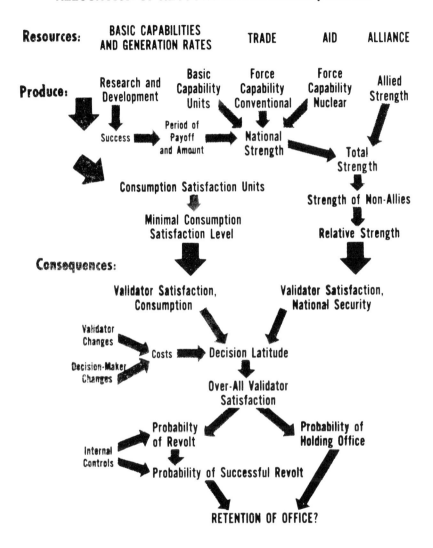

Figure taken from Crow, W.J. A study of strategic doctrines using the Inter-
Nation Simulation. J. Conflict Resolut., 1963 (September), 7, page 582.

The decision-makers have access to four types of resources: the nation's "basic capabilities," and trade, aid, and alliances. At the beginning of the run, each nation starts with a specific amount of "basic capability," representing the entire range of its resources, both physical and human. This variable is the analog of national wealth and as such establishes the nation's relative position along a dimension from "poor" to "wealthy."

Each nation is also assigned "generation-rates" which determine the amount of goods and services that can be produced with one unit of basic capability. Within each nation there are different generation rates for the production of (1) additional basic capability units, (2) consumer satisfaction units, (3) conventional, or (4) nuclear-force capabilities. Through investment in specific research and development projects, the CDM can designate which generation-rate he wishes to improve, but the Simulation Director decides, through a probabilistic determination, whether, and when a project will pay off. These generation-rates, differing from nation to nation in the model, are the analog of "economic development"; thus they establish the relative position of each nation along a dimension ranging from "underdeveloped" to "highly developed."

A nation's decision-makers can negotiate with other nations in their world, and can enter into agreements with them, making maximal use of the law of comparative advantage through judicious choices among selective aid, trade, and alliance-formation. Favorable arrangements of this sort may result in a greater fund of commodities or basic capability units, and/or enhanced domestic tranquility or international power.

Decisions as to the allocation of these four types of resources -- basic capability, trade, aid, and alliances -- produce certain intermediate developments in the operation of the simulation, as shown on Figure 1.

Resources may be internally invested in five major ways: (1) in research and development projects, as mentioned above; or for the direct production of (2) additional basic capability units (analogous to the production of capital goods); or (3) conventional force capability units; or (4) nuclear capability units; or (5) "consumer satisfaction" units (analogous to consumer goods).

Allocation of resources to the production of either basic capability units or force-capability units increases the nation's strength; its strength together with the strength of its allies, determines the total strength of the nation (see Figure 1). A nation's relative strength in the model world is, of course, a function of the strength of the next strongest bloc.

Moving farther down on Figure 1, it may be seen that the allocation of resources has consequences with respect to the nation's "validators" -- the analog of "public opinion," elite pressure groups, or vested interests -- who validate a decision-maker's choices and thus exert considerable influence over his decisions.

"Validator satisfaction," as Figure 1 shows, is determined by two parameters: "consumption," and "national security." The level of consumption units remaining in the nation at the end of each period, above that required for minimal subsistence, determines the "consumption satisfaction" of the validators; satisfaction with respect to national security is a function of the nation's relative strength within the international system. Calculations of validator-satisfaction for each nation, however, must incorporate the effect of "international" decisions, that is, internal modifications of one nation's total strength may have immediate and even profound repercussions on any other nation's level of validator-satisfaction with respect to national security.

In brief, we have seen so far that decisions regarding the allocation of resources determine the nation's growth and strength, which in turn affect the satisfaction of its validators.

The final operations, diagrammed on the lower portion of Figure 1, apply to the domestic political scene, and directly affect the probability that the CDM will or will not retain office.

Each CDM begins the simulation with a specified degree of "decision latitude," which tells him how responsive he must be to his validators. Changes in decision-latitude, however, may be initiated either by the validators or by the CDM himself. But if he initiates changes which conflict with the wishes of his validators -- if, for example, he demands greater latitude, while his validators wish it maintained at its current level, or decreased -- he must pay a cost: since basic capability units represent human resources (including morale) as well as physical, his fund of basic capability units is proportionately decreased.

Decision-latitude level influences the calculations, made during each period, of over-all validator-satisfaction, on which depends the CDM's likelihood of retaining office. The latter is calculated periodically for either of two conditions: orderly transfer of power (analogous to elections), or disorderly change (rebellion, revolution). Should the level of over-all validator-satisfaction fall below a predetermined "revolution-threshold," and if insufficient force-capability units have been allotted for maintaining internal control, then disorderly change -- a coup d'etat, revolution or assassination -- may follow. Upon losing office, the CDM exchange roles with the Aspiring Central Decision-Maker.

To summarize: the decision-makers in the Inter-Nation Simulation are confronted with a complex, interrelated system of variables and processes within which they must interpose their judgment at a variety of choice-points. Many of the consequences of these decisions are programmed by the Simulation Director on the basis of formulae and quantitative interrelationships predetermined by the INS model.

A major advantage of this type of man-computer simulation is that although the participants must operate within the constraints imposed by the structured program, they are allowed a broad range of "free activity" (see Guetzkow, 1963). This represents, for the most part, the operation of such "intangible" psychological variables as individual philosophies of international relations, as well as individual

41

motives and interests, systems of values or ethics, modes of perceiving and judging, all of which influence the development of attitudes toward others within the system -- in itself one of the most crucial psychological variables. It is from this domain of "real" psychological variables that many of the unique and behaviorally rich contributions of the INS have arisen.

It should be apparent that in order to collect data from such an ongoing system, the experimenter need only "plug in" appropriate instruments at various points during the operation. Thus, all face-to-face meetings and conferences can be tape-recorded for later study, and all written communications are retained for analysis; a "newspaper, " issued periodically during the life of the simulation, both gives the participants information about current events in their world, and provides data for the experimenter. In addition, rating scales, questionnaires, open-ended essay-questions, etc., may be administered during the simulation, whenever it is germane to the research. A review of some INS studies, presented below, will illustrate how data are generated and recorded by means of this particular simulation technique.

Some Recent INS Findings

In discussing the following studies, I shall only indicate the research concerns of each, and outline the major findings.

One of the earliest investigations employing the INS as a research tool was that of Driver (1962). Among other things, he was interested in examining the effects of situational stress on the way participants perceive other "nations" in their model "world." Driver hypothesized that a curvilinear relationship would be found between situational stress and the conceptual complexity of individual perceptions of other "nations." The experiment is described as follows:

A total of 357 Middle Western high school students of both sexes participated in the different runs of the INS. Each run involved seven simulated nations, each manned by three subjects performing specified roles for a four-day period. The runs which eventuated in simulated wars were classified as providing intense stress. Peacetime runs were subdivided into the moderately stressful and mildly stressful. The complexity of the subjects' concepts of the simulated nations was evaluated in terms of differentiation, integration, and other attributes of the conceptual structure. It was pointed out that the more complex concepts permit a fuller and more balanced consideration of all relevant variables and hence facilitate effective decision making. (in Anastasi, 1964, p. 573)

The hypothesis was substantiated by the data: i.e., the most complex concepts were found under conditions of intermediate stress. These findings suggest that as situational stress increases in international relations, the likelihood of effective decision-making tends to decrease. Thus it may be that when international tension levels rise -- the very time when excellence is most required in international decision-making -- the existence of stress itself may tend to reduce the complexity of the decision-makers' perceptions to a "black-and-white, " "either-or" level, and lessen the efficacy of the decision-making process.

In a recent study at Northwestern University (Robinson, Hermann, and Hermann, in Higgs and Weinland, 1964, pp. 41-42) the INS was used specifically to investigate the process of "crisis" decision-making:

The purpose of this study is twofold: first to examine the value of an a priori definition of crisis as a type of decision situation or occasion; and second, to test the relationship between crisis and variables such as personality, decision behavior, and organizational lines of authority...

A series of ten runs of seven periods each will be conducted. The "world" in each run will have eight nations -- two alliances of three nations each and two neutral nations. Six of these nations will have five officeholders each. A Central Decision-Maker will act as head of government. Under him are the Internal Decision-Maker, the External Decision-Maker, and the Force Decision-Maker. An Aspiring Decision-Maker represents the opposing elites in the nation and seeks to gain control of the government. The other two nations are confederate nations to the experimenter, and each is run by two persons. These four individuals, plus the Newspaper Editor, the International Organization Chairman, and the Simulation Director (all members of the experimental staff) will introduce the crisis problems into each "world. "

The independent variable, crisis, will be defined in terms of three dimensions: (1) a threat to major goals; (2) a short decision-time available for response; and (3) a lack of anticipation by the decision-makers that the threatening situation may transpire, i. e. , an element of surprise. (op. cit. , p. 41)

Preliminary results, based upon six INS runs and an analysis of 70% of the data, reveal the following tendencies: A hypothesis that information is more likely to be sought in crisis than in non-crisis situations was not supported; there appeared to be little search for information for either crisis or non-crisis decisions. However, the results tend to support a hypothesis that where there is less information-search in crisis than in non-crisis situations, it is more likely to be due to time pressures that limit the search than because the situation is already well-defined. A highly significant finding of this study is that in a crisis, as contrasted with a non-crisis, it is more likely that only one or two available courses of action will be perceived, rather than a variety of alternatives. This result nicely corroborates Driver's earlier finding that cognitive complexity decreases under

43

stress. Moreover, the present study supports the hypothesis that in a crisis, as contrasted with a non-crisis, there will be less search for alternatives. However, a more detailed analysis of the data shows that to the extent search behavior does occur in a crisis, there is more search for information than for alternatives.

It seems reasonable to assume that the nature of the crisis might produce differences in decision behavior, and this was confirmed with respect to the distribution of authority. When non-crisis situations were contrasted with all types of crises, it was found that authority contracts in a crisis, i. e., that fewer individuals are involved in the decision process. However, this did not hold true when the crisis was an unidentified military attack; in this case, the most frequent immediate reaction was to convene all the nation's decision-makers.

The experimenters hypothesized that in a crisis, persons in ascribed authority roles will be more likely to exercise influence than will those whose authority is based on expertise, but this was not supported by the results. Other of the preliminary findings from this study suggest that under crisis conditions: (1) the use of both domestic and foreign human resources is curtailed; and (2) the decision outcome increases the risk that objectives will not be attained, either because no action at all is taken, or because the action taken increases the hostility between the adversaries. If these findings apply in the "real world, " it is clear that a nation which is aware of, and can counteract such detrimental crisis behaviors, might thus be better enabled to meet situations of high tension constructively.

The reduction of international tensions was specifically investigated by Solomon and Crow (Solomon, 1963; Crow, 1963; Crow and Solomon, 1962), using the Inter-Nation Simulation. In a pilot study these investigators asked: Could a series of friendly acts by one major power toward another major power reduce international tensions and increase prospects for world peace? The simulated world was structured as a prototype of the bi-polar, "Cold War" world of 1960; the investigators intervened in the simulation by instructing one of the nations to follow a strategy specifically designed to reduce international tensions -- Charles Osgood's "GRIT" -- Graduated and Reciprocated Initiative in Tension-Reduction (Osgood, 1962). GRIT calls for a nation to initiate a series of unilateral actions, graduated over time from low to high risk, which are designed to be seen by the opponent as threat-reducing. Reciprocation is invited, but each act is unconditional. Moreover, these unilateral actions are of a kind that do not endanger the basic security of the initiating nation.

In its dealings with other nations, OMNE, the prototype of the United States, was instructed to pursue a strategy designed to first increase tensions in the world, and then decrease them. Tension was periodically measured with simple rating scales on which the participants indicated their opinion as to the likelihood of war, and their perception of the trust-level and the amount of tension in the simulated world. The data were plotted immediately, enabling the experimenters to keep tabs on the tension level at any given time and accordingly to instruct the CDM of OMNE, secretly, as to his next move.

44

Figure 2 shows the changes in tension level during the 13 periods of this simulation. As may be seen, tension level was clearly correlated with OMNE's actions; tension built to a peak following such tension-inducing moves as an arms build-up, discriminatory aid and trade agreements, and the proliferation of nuclear armaments within the OMNE alliance. Tension abruptly decreased after GRIT was introduced at the end of period 7, and, in general, continued to fall until the simulation ended.

Crow and Raser more recently undertook a similar study entitled, "The Capacity to Delay Response: The Deterrent Effectiveness of a Weapons Posture," (in Higgs and Weinland, 1964, pp. 92-93). The central hypothesis of this study was that a nation's known capacity to delay response to a nuclear attack increases the stability of a deterrence situation. A nation with an invulnerable retaliatory capacity can gather and evaluate information after it has been attacked, and can thus more effectively choose the nature and timing of its response.

The Crow-Raser study was designed to examine the effect of this known option upon international perceptions and relations. The following hypotheses were tested: (1) A nation with the capacity to delay response (CDR) will be perceived as stronger but less threatening than one without it; (2) such a nation will be able to negotiate more adequately and will have greater deterrent capability; (3) in a deterrence system where one nuclear power is known to have CDR, as compared to one in which no nation has it, the probability of accidental, catalytic, or preemptive war will be less, interest in arms control agreements will be less, alliance cohesion will be less, probability of strategic war will be reduced, and the wars that do occur will be more limited.

Results from 12 runs of this simulation, each consisting of 15 periods, indicate that: Contrary to expectation, when one nation gains CDR, intended strategic wars occur more frequently and are of greater magnitude, primarily because the CDR nation itself tends to start wars; CDR increases both that nation's perceived strength and the amount of threat it presents. Interest in arms control agreements tends to go down in the CDR nation, but goes up in the others; CDR does not affect that nation's negotiating ability, but tends to increase its deterrent capacity; cohesion of the CDR nation's alliances is not affected, but the cohesion of opposing alliances tends to decrease. On the other hand, CDR decreases the probability of accidental, catalytic, or preemptive war; i.e., CDR decreases the probability of unintended strategic war.

Validity Studies of the INS

If the INS technique is to be used as a source of behavioral science information for students of international affairs, the relation between its findings and "real world" events must be established. But as Snyder has pointed out,

At this stage in the development of the social sciences, and especially at this stage in the development of simulation

FIGURE 2

GENERAL TENSION LEVEL: CDM-MEANS OF
ALL NATIONS AND ALL SCALES

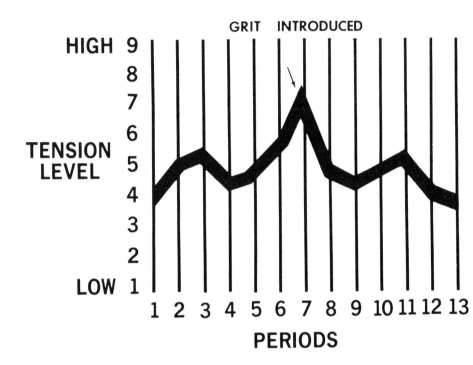

Figure taken from Crow, W.J. A study of strategic doctrines using the Inter-

Nation Simulation. J. Conflict Resolut., 1963 (September), 7, page 588.

techniques for analyzing international relations, most experiments belong in the discover phase of science-building, not in the verification phase. (Snyder, in Guetzkow, et al., 1963, p. 7)

Despite many similar cautions that emphasis should be placed on the heuristic use of simulation research, increasingly the technique has been used to generate findings assumed to have some predictive value for events in the real world. It is evident that the external validity of INS findings depends on the correspondence between the INS model and the empirical reality which it purports to represent. To date, attempts have been made to verify the ecological generality of the INS model in three ways: by structuring the model in such a way as to see how well it recreates a known historical outcome, parallels ongoing present events, or what it predicts with respect to a plausible future situation. Three studies, each employing one of these approaches, are briefly reviewed below.

Charles and Margaret Hermann (Hermann and Hermann, 1963) assumed that confidence in the model's capacity to predict future events would be enhanced if it could be shown that the model would reproduce known events of the past with reasonable adequacy.

The Hermanns undertook to simulate events leading to the outbreak of World War I, attempting, also, to match the personalities of INS participants with those of the real world leaders involved in the summer crisis of 1914. Drawing heavily on a Stanford University analysis of the European political situation in 1914, they conducted two exploratory runs to see whether the data from this historical situation would validate the basic framework of the simulation.

On a macroanalytic level, the results were encouraging: although neither run eventuated in war, there were some convergences with historical realities. On a microanalytic level, a correlation of .80 was found between content analyses of messages sent in the simulation and those actually sent in the summer of 1914. This correlation was not significant, however, due to the small size of the $\underline{N}$, and further replications are necessary to increase confidence in these findings.

A study designed to see whether the INS can parallel current real world events is presently under way under the direction of Dorothy Meier (Meier, 1963). The general strategy of this project is to design the simulation in correspondence with the real world situation at a concurrent point in time, and then to run the simulated system ahead, on a telescoped time-dimension, for a period equivalent to one year of real world time. Unfolding events in the real world can then be compared to events in the simulation. As a further refinement, aimed at clarifying the predictability of the INS, "panels of experts" (social scientists, news analysts, etc.) will be intensively interviewed as to their best predictions of the course of international events during the time-period covered by the simulation. The "educated guesses" of these experts will be compared with the "predictions" obtained by the INS runs, and both will be compared with actual events in the real world. Findings from this study are not yet available.

Brody (1963) has employed the third, predictive, approach to the problem of validation in his study of the spread of nuclear weapons technology. Confronted with the uncertainties posed by a world of many, rather than few nuclear powers, Brody undertook to see what a controlled manipulation of the INS might yield with respect to the "n-country" problem.

His simulated world began as a cold-war system composed of two hierarchically organized bloc-alliances in which the leading nation of each possessed a virtual monopoly over nuclear force capabilities. He hypothesized that the spread of nuclear capability in the simulation would produce a change in the alliance structure. Data from 17 runs, using students as decision-makers, confirmed the hypothesis. After all countries had achieved nuclear capability (the "n-country" situation), tensions within each bloc increased, at the same time that bloc cohesion decreased. There were significant changes in communication patterns, reflecting the fragmentation of the original blocs. Future developments in the real world, some of which have already occurred, will help establish the validity of these simulation predictions.

## Other Uses of Simulation Techniques

It should be apparent from the preceding that the simulation techniques may serve for a variety of purposes. Its use in research allows the controlled, experimental investigation of complex systems and processes, and the technique itself has valuable heuristic features which may lead to the discovery of significant variables in the real world -- variables which are not, at present, amenable to more direct methods of investigation. Simulation can be used to build a variety of models other than the Inter-Nation: e. g., self-contained societies, from primitive to highly complex; organizations (business, community, religious, etc.); or even family or small-group situations.

Already, simulation has shown itself to be a potentially valuable pedagogical tool in various teaching and training programs. Participation in the INS is, for the subjects, a dynamic experience; it endows many concepts of international relations with strict and technical meaning as compared with the abstract, dramatic, or literary quality they have for most students.

A preliminary comparison between students in a case-study section and those in a simulation section did not show clear-cut advantages for either. However, students in the simulation-section were more involved, and found the course more interesting; participation, attendance, and course-evaluations were higher, and there was more student-to-student feedback (Anderson, et al., 1964). There is evident need for further and more detailed research in this area.

## Phenomenological World of the Participants

There is a seeming paradox in the developing use of simulation for research in international relations. Whereas the origins and the rationale of the technique are strongly grounded in the behavioristic tradition, the external validity of this approach depends on whether it is phenomenologically isomorphic with the real world decision-making environments which it proposes to simulate. Thus, it is being recognized, increasingly, that the subjective perceptions of the participants are primary determinants of decisional behavior.

Accordingly, some of the most pressing questions now confronting INS experimenters concern the phenomenological world of the participants: e. g. , on what sort of self-instructions do participants base their decisional-behavior -- what values, philosophies, concepts of "human nature, " influence them? How does the CDM perceive his validators, and toward what objectives do these perceptions tend to push him? How do values and ideological orientations develop or change in the context of the simulation experience, and what are the determinants of these cognitive modifications? How does the "self-concept" (as the origin of phenomenological anxieties, purposes, and desires) influence decisional behavior in the simulation -- i. e. , determine the perception and meaning of "threat, " relate to the expansion and contraction of time perspective in various situations, and condition responses to the variety of programmed and unprogrammed occurrences?

## Suggested Modifications

Many other questions face those engaged in simulation-research, but a fundamental problem, as was suggested earlier in this paper, is that of validity. The need for cross-cultural testing of results is of course obvious, for a simulated international system is clearly incomplete if it does not incorporate some analogs of the cultural, social, and ethnic differences that exist in real international systems.

Several cross-cultural simulation studies have already been made, one using foreign embassy personnel in Washington as participants, one using foreign students at Northwestern University, and a third, carried out by Crow and Raser, using Mexican students at the National University of Mexico. In the latter study (Crow & Raser, 1964), results were compared to those obtained with American Navy recruits. With respect to the major variable, Capacity to Delay Response, results with both groups were strikingly similar; there were also similarities in the way both groups responded to their own participation in the simulation, and to certain of its events. On the other hand, there were some interesting differences: Mexican participants exchanged 60-70% more messages than did the United States participants, and put more emphasis on form (diplomatic phrasing, grammar, etc. ) than on content; Mexican subjects placed more emphasis on international issues -- peace, disarmament, and the International Organization (analog of the U. N. ); steadfastly resisted being drawn into an arms race. They showed little concern with internal economic growth; the Mexican CDMs shared power to a greater degree; and responses to a questionnaire indicate that the Mexican participants reactions to stress and frustration were passive rather than active.

It would be exceedingly worthwhile to carry out cross-cultural

INS studies in as broad a spectrum of social and cultural settings as possible; plans are already under way for INS projects in Japan and in Europe.

However, the heart of the validity question for INS research is this: How close is the correspondence between the significant elements in the phenomenal world of the simulation, and the significant elements in the phenomenal world of international decision-makers? To answer this question, it is essential that genotypical social-psychological processes be incorporated in the INS operating model -- but to do so, we must know whether such research produces genotypical or phenotypical results, a question which can be answered only by further research and extended replication. Moreover, as Newcomb has pointed out, the discovery of genotypical laws and principles must await a taxonomy of Phenotypes (Newcomb, 1951). In social psychology, the differentiating and labeling process has scarcely begun; the INS might well contribute to this taxonomic endeavor, in the course of attempting to identify the genotypical processes necessary for the creation of a valid model.

## The INS and Peace Theory

At the conclusion of his book, Peace Theory: Preconditions of Disarmament, Burton says:

> It has been assumed that the unsystematized study of international relations was dealing broadly with the study of peaceful relationships. But as we have seen, the studies which purport to be studies relating to peace are in fact studies of political warfare, of military strategy, of international organization, of power balances, and of other enforcement devices. There has been no endeavor, so far as one can ascertain, to develop a study which would be concerned with peaceful relationships. (Burton, 1963, p. 197)

This indictment, painfully true not only of general research on international relations, but even of most INS studies, might be partially met by making certain modifications in the INS conceptual model. One suggestion, for example, is that a Decision-Maker for Peace be included, to act in conjunction with the traditional decision-makers. This should enable the experimenter to explore many different policy alternatives for achieving a peaceful international system, as well as to see what sorts of relationships develop between a decisional office-holder explicitly committed to peace, and the more traditionally-oriented bureaucracies.

Burton's proposed Peace Theory envisages a world in which foreign policy is characterized by neutralism and non-discrimination, and international organization is characterized by functionalism and regionalism. Such a foreign policy involves "states of mind" in the decision-makers, and could easily be introduced in the INS. Various degrees of functionalism could be programmed into INS organizations with little difficulty. Finally, regionalism could be incorporated, within limits, by the introduction of a geography -- an element which the INS so far has lacked.

In this connection, it is interesting that during an INS run with diplomatic personnel as participants, many spontaneously commented on this lack, and expressed a need for some kind of conceptual map which would enable them to relate the nations geographically.

In conclusion, then, serious exploration of a Peace Theory requires, first of all, that we explore the concept of peace, not as the mere absence of war, but as a "condition" or phenomenological "situation" with its own unique dimensions and requirements of which Man has had little experience and hence has little knowledge. Simulation techniques -- and particularly the Inter-Nation Simulation -- appear to offer an exceedingly fruitful method for exploring the phenomenon of peace.

## Summary

This paper describes the Inter-Nation Simulation, an experimental technique that enables decision-making processes to be studied within the constraints of a simulated international system.

The nature and operation of the INS are delineated, together with an analysis of the economic, political, and military variables programmed into the functioning model; unprogrammed socio-psychological variables which influence the results are also discussed. Several studies based on the INS are briefly reviewed, and the central question of validity is explored. Modifications of the current conceptual model are suggested, with implication for the development of an integrated Peace Theory.

## References

Anastasi, A. Fields of applied psychology. New York: McGraw-Hill, 1964, p. 573.

Anderson, L., Hermann, M., Robinson, J. and Snyder, R. A Comparison of simulation, case studies, and problem papers in teaching decision-making. Evanston, Ill., Northwestern University, 1964. (mimeographed report).

Brody, R. A. Some systemic effects of the spread of nuclear weapons technology: A study through simulation of a multi-nuclear future. J. Conflict Resolut., 1963 (December), 7, 663-753.

Burton, J. Peace theory: Preconditions of disarmament. New York: Alfrd Knopf, 1962.

Crow, W. J. and Solomon, L. N. A simulation study of strategic doctrines. La Jolla, Calif.: Western Behavioral Sciences Institute, 1962. (dittoed report).

Crow, W. J. A study of strategic doctrines using the Inter-Nation Simulation. J. Conflict Resolut., 1963 (September, 7, 580-589.

Crow, W. J. Simulation: The construction and use of functioning models in international relations. La Jolla, Calif., Western Behavioral Sciences Institute, 1964. (dittoed report).

Crow, W. J. and Raser, J. R. A cross-cultural simulation study. La Jolla, Calif., Western Behavioral Sciences Institute, 1964. (dittoed report).

Driver, M. Conceptual structure and group processes in an internation simulation. Educ. Test. Serv., RB-62-15, April, 1962.

Guetzkow, H. (Ed.) Simulation in social science: Readings. Englewood Cliffs, N. J. Prentice Hall, 1962.

Guetzkow, H., Alger, C., Brody, R., Noel, R. and Snyder, R. Simulation in international relations: Developments for research and teaching. Englewood Cliffs, N. J. Prentice Hall, 1963.

Hermann, C. and Hermann, M. Validation studies of the inter-nation simulation. China Lake, Calif. U.S. Naval Ordnance Test Station, TP 3351, December 1963.

Higgs, L. and Weinland, R. Project Michelson Status Report 1. China Lake, Calif. U.S. Naval Ordnance Test Station, TP 3448, April 1964.

Meier, D. Progress report: Event simulation project (INS-16). Evanston, Ill. International Relations Program, Northwestern University, November 1963. (dittoed report).

Newcomb, T. "Social psychological theory: Integrating individual and social approaches." In Rohrer, J. and Sherif, M. Social psychology at the crossroads. New York: Harper, 1951.

Osgood, C. E. An alternative to war or surrender. Urbana, Ill. University of Illinois Press, 1962.

Snyder, R. "Some perspectives on the use of experimental techniques in the study of international relations" In Guetzkow, et al, Simulation in International Relations: Developments for research and teaching. Englewood Cliffs, N. J. Prentice Hall, 1963, p. 1-23.

Solomon, L. N. Reducing tensions in a test-tube world. War/Peace Report, 1963 (July), 3, 10-12: also in Naval Research Reviews, 1963 (November, 16, 17-20 & 33).

# INTERNATIONAL RELATIONS AS A BEHAVIORAL SCIENCE:
## PROBLEMS, APPROACHES AND FINDINGS

Richard A. Brody
Stanford University

As I understand it, this symposium is concerned with the role of psychology in the study of international politics; this timely topic has been the subject of heated public debate (Jordan, 1963; Sawyer, 1963; McNeil, 1963) and autobiographical soul searching (Osgood, 1964) by psychologists. As a political scientist, I have very little desire to enter the hustings of an intra-disciplinary quarrel -- I prefer to study conflict between nations. However, as a behavioral scientist concerned with international conflict I cannot avoid coming to grips with some of the central issues of this debate.

Two of these issues are fundamental to any scientific approach to the study of international politics and have been hotly debated in political science as well as psychology. I have reference, of course, to problems dealing with the generalizing of findings about one sphere of social relations (or other aspects of human behavior) to another sphere and to the prior question, "what are the behaving (acting) units in international politics, i. e. , who are the actors?"

I will try to briefly state my position on these two questions and, having done this, turn to the main concern of this paper: the examination of problems, approaches, and research findings which currently characterize behavioral science research in international politics.

The choice of a unit of analysis for studying international relations is entirely arbitrary. Each level of aggregation or organization (e. g. , nation-states, populations, or decision-making groups) can be considered a potentially useful choice but for different research tasks. Each alternative, moreover, carries with it potential advantages and disadvantages and its own peculiar set of assumptions which the analyst must adopt with his choice of a research focus (Wolfers, 1962).

The Stanford Studies in International Conflict and Integration have joined those of our fellow political scientists who are concentrating on individuals, in the context of decision-making roles, as the focal point of analysis. We have done this on the assumption that individual and group factors have relevance for the explanation of foreign policy behavior.

Those who select the nation-state as the focus of analysis have either assumed that there is no variance in psychological factors, i. e. , that all "nations" have the same attitudes and motivations (Wolfers, 1962, p. 10), or that the "national psychology" is that represented by the "character" of the nation (Klineberg, 1964). Jordan seems to have joined the "nations-as-actors" school when he asserts, "the term, 'international relations' refers to entities like nations, governments, armed forces" (1963, p. 29), but his article can also be read as an attack on this point of view.

The point of all of this is that irrespective of which unit of analysis is chosen, psychological assumptions are unavoidable (this is the case, because we are dealing with social processes involving people). It also illustrates the point that we are better off if these assumptions are made explicit.

The second central issue involves generalizing behavioral regularities from one domain of social interaction to another. Jordan (1963) is particularly vociferous on this point. It seems to me remarkably unproductive to stand on either side of the issue shouting "you can!" "you can't!" The issue is far more subtle than the public debate would indicate; it involves an area which has received precious little attention from philosophers of science whose sober judgment is sorely needed.

Those of us who yearn for laws of human behavior which are not markedly sensitive to system size or complexity can take some comfort from Zetterberg's assertion that regularities observed at one level of social organization are more likely to obtain at other levels than are their opposites (1963, p. 53). However, even Zetterberg acknowledges that this is a difficult proposition to prove. Perhaps the safest procedure is to hypothesize that a behavioral regularity in one domain of human behavior will also be found to hold in international relations and then seek an empirical test for the hypothesis -- hardly a novel procedure, but one not often followed.

The points of view I have expressed on these two issues are not the only ones which will be held by those doing systematic research in international relations. They do not, moreover, point to any single approach to the subject matter of international politics. These remarks are intended to clarify some of the motivation behind our research activity.

### The Focus on Man in Context

The intellectual ferment, which characterizes the modern study of international politics, stems from a disarmingly simple insight: international politics, like any social activity, involves people. It follows, if people are involved in operating the international system, that individual, group, and organizational psychological factors may aid in explaining the behavior men, organized into nations, exhibit toward each other.

The top foreign policy leaders of a nation are not just men -- they are men in socially defined roles which may constrain their behavior. Neither are they merely decision-making machines which weigh "national interest" and "national power" against the opportunity for "national gain" to arrive at policy. National leaders are individuals making policy choices for their nations in a complex of highly articulated group, organizational, societal, and inter-societal systems. The task of the behavioral scientist studying international politics is to gain understanding of how these systems fit together and how they affect the choice behavior of individuals in leadership roles.

But herein we come upon the fundamental dilemma of international relations as a behavioral science: If we study individuals stripped of this system context, what will we learn of their behavior in context? On the other hand, if we attempt to study them in context, how do we gain access to them?

The psychologist who is interested in behavioral principles which are not context bound has available to him an arsenal of assessment instruments most of which require for their application direct contact with, or observation of the subject. But how can we give a Taylor Manifest Anxiety Scale to Khrushchev during the Hungarian revolt, or a Semantic Differential to Chiang Kai-shek while Quemoy is being shelled? Occasionally behavioral scientists can gain direct access to decision-makers -- usually during periods of relative calm -- but direct access is out of the question with all but a few historical figures, whose behavior provides a rich source of case material.

The requirement of doing analysis at a distance (removed in time and/or space from our "subjects") has opened the student of international politics to the charge of being inordinately self-conscious about method -- whether to an inordinate or appropriate extent is a matter of opinion. Several recent publications have a decidedly "how to do it" cast (e. g. , Guetzkow, et al. , 1963; North, et al. , 1963; Holsti, et al. , 1964) but they are also concerned with "why to do it. " Much of this work is offered in the spirit of attempting to interest other scholars in one or another "approach" and thus spread the task of building a cumulative body of empirical research. In this respect we differ little from any science.

Recognition of the problems of doing analyses at a distance and the epistemological shortcomings of any one approach has had a salutory effect on the interchange among scholars in this field. Researchers emphasizing one approach openly encourage those employing other methods and much research involves multi-method, multi-trait analyses.

The problem of access has been approached in a number of ways: (1) through aggregate data analyses, (2) through direct access to analogous situations, and (3) through indirect analyses of actual situations. We are too close to the beginning of these efforts to know whether the hoped for convergence of findings will occur, but neither are we like the proverbial blind man -- unaware that we are working over the same beast.

Those who emphasize the aggregate data approach are basically concerned with two problems: determining the typical interaction patterns among types of nations, and ascertaining the factors predicting the direction of changing relationships among nations.

There are over 120 nations capable of carrying on some sort of international relations (that means over 7 thousand dyads and endless triads and tetrads). On the assumption that not all of the differences which distinguish these nations are relevant for their international politics, there have been undertaken a series of studies which seek to establish the minimum number of factors describing nations which yield the maximum explanatory power in describing their interrelations with other nations (Deutsch, 1960; Rummel, 1963). This is analogous to investigating whether sex, age, I. Q. , and the like, predict relations in a school setting -- a familiar sociological approach. The yield of this research will be a systematic taxonomy of nation-types and evidence on within-type and between-type relations.

Karl Deutsch and his associates have also used aggregate data analyses to explain the waxing and waning of alliances and to test Deutsch's theory of the conditions under which different degrees of coalition emerge (Deutsch, 1954; Deutsch, et al. , 1956; Russett, 1963).

There is an explicit psychological dimension to Deutsch's work; it involves the relationship between the quantity and quality of mutual perceptions, and the degree of integration (1954, pp. 33ff. ). Russett (1963) has employed Deutsch's approach to chart the focus of attention in the anglo-American dyad (since 1900); his study can aid us to explain the evident lack of mutual responsiveness which has increasingly come to characterize the alliance since 1956.

Rummel (1963; 1964) has employed factor analysis and multi-variate analysis of aggregate data to determine the relationship between domestic and international conflict (it is a surprisingly weak one) and to select predictors of both types of conflict. His findings can be interpreted to emphasize the potential relevance of psychological variables in the explanation of international conflict. He reports ". . . the predictor variables have some success in accounting for a lack or for low levels of . . . conflict behavior, but are generally unable to account for high magnitudes in the occurrence of such behavior (1964, p. 93). " This departure from linearity corresponds to preliminary findings that perceptual variables account for variance to the degree that national leaders feel their nations are involved in a crisis situation (Holsti, et al. , 1964; Zaninovich, 1964). This correspondence is certainly not conclusive, but suggests the need for combining aggregate data and perceptual data approaches. [1] Some of this has already been done by those emphasizing the direct approach to individuals in analogous situations (Guetzkow, et al. , 1963; Brody, 1963; Crow, 1963; Raser and Crow, 1964).

The idea of doing research in an analogous social system (field or laboratory), so familiar to psychologists, is a relatively new approach for students of international politics. The logic of this approach is simple, but the execution is difficult and not devoid of hazard.

The logic of the approach calls for building into the simulate enough of the contextual elements found in the actual system so that behavior observed in the simulate will validly replicate behavior observed in the actual system. If this is accomplished or substantially approximated, the rewards are rich indeed. Multiple replications of the same situation can be accomplished which can serve to increase our understanding of the interrelation of situational, psychological and outcome variables; the effect on probable future situations can be examined in advance of their emergence in the actual system (e. g. , Brody, 1963; Raser and Crow, 1964); the effect of psychological variables (attitudes, cognitions, personality, etc. ) can be directly assessed by standardized techniques.

Harold Guetzkow and his associates at Northwestern are currently doing a substantial amount of research on the validity of the inter-nation simulation. This includes prediction studies of the near future (a kind of goodness-of-fit test) and runs with subjects who are actual diplomats (tests for cross-cultural and cross-experience level stabilities). I am enthusiastic about the results that Charles and Margaret Hermann (1963) obtained in their attempt to validate the simulation against historical data.

Simulations have been used to examine the spread of nuclear weapons (Brody, 1963), the effect of strategic doctrines on international stability (Crow and Solomon, 1962; Crow, 1963), effects of weapon system characteristics on national policy (Raser and Crow, 1964), and the effects of three kinds of stress on decision-making (Robinson and Hermann, 1964). All of these studies indicate the relevance of psychological variables in the complex inter-group processes present in the inter-nation simulation. The results of the validation experiments (if they are positive) will add to our confidence that similar findings can be expected in the actual international system.

The third "approach" (i. e. , indirect access to actual situations) has proceeded on two distinguishable paths: (1) the retrospective reconstruction of decision processes and (2) the analysis of manifest content to determine underlying attitudes. These solutions to the problems of analysis at a distance are generally called "decision-making analysis" (Snyder, et al. , 1962) and "content analysis" (North, et al. , 1963; Holsti, et al. , 1964) respectively.

The "decision-making approach, " typified by the work of Snyder and his associates (Snyder, et al. , 1962; Snyder and Paige, 1958) has relied heavily on the retrospective reports of actual participants as to whom and what was involved in a given foreign policy decision. The interviews in which these reports are developed are constructed so as to focus attention on motivation, perceptions of the situation, group and organizational process, the sources of initiative and alternatives, and like topics. Throughout this work there is a conscious effort to gauge the relevance of psychological studies of decision-making. Snyder refers to the attempt to "embrace two levels of analysis in a single framework -- the sociological level (organizational factors) and the psychological level (individual or personality factors)" as a "central feature" of his analytic scheme (1963, p. 243).

The many findings in the Korean case study point to the conclusion that decision-making in crisis takes place in the presence of psychological and organizational simplification: The decision tends to be made by a small face-to-face group of top leaders which insulates itself from the wider organizational setting. The tendency is to consider few, rather than many, alternatives; perceptions tend to be focussed on figure rather than ground, and so forth. Pruitt's research on decision-making in the Department of State (1962 and 1964-65) would tend to support Snyder's findings.

There are difficulties attendant to the retrospective interview approach. Two seem particularly relevant in the present context: (1) access to decision-makers is largely restricted to one side of the cold war dyad, (2) the dependence on recall in self-reporting is a formidable source of error variance. The first difficulty, of course, disappears if the decision was taken by a nation to whose leaders the analyst has access. The difficulties with recall data have been overcome by supplementing these data with materials not produced retrospectively -- diaries, speeches, etc. Nevertheless, awareness of these difficulties has led to an alternative approach -- the content analysis of verbal and written materials contemporaneous to the decision and originating with the decision-makers.

"Content analysis" has been described by Charles Osgood as "attempts to infer the characteristics and intentions of sources from inspection of the messages they produce" (1957, p. 275). Several scholars have used one or another variant of content analysis to, as it were, gain access without contact. Snyder and Paige (1958) studied the United States' decision to resist aggression in Korea in part by interviewing participants. Whiting (1960), who was interested in the Chinese decision to enter the same conflict, but barred from contact with Chinese leadership, depended upon content analysis for data on the decision process.

The Stanford Studies in International Conflict and Integration, under the direction of Robert North, turned to the use of content measures when the importance of psychological factors in the understanding of the development of international crises became palpable. The work of Charles McClelland on the "crisis interaction process" (e.g., 1961), the decision-making studies, and our own preliminary research on the 1914 crisis (Zinnes, et al., 1961) pointed to the need to tap decision-makers' perceptions in seeking to explain their policy behavior. Content analysis seems to us the most practical means of developing assessments of decision-makers' perceptual responses which are comparable for contemporary and historical situations for any nation (however situated with respect to the cold war), and for regional as well as general conflict situations.

Using content analysis, we have been able to establish the catalytic role that perceptions of hostility played in the 1914 crisis (Holsti, et al., 1964), and the strong relationship between perceptions of hostility and feelings of involvement of Soviet and Chinese leaders in three contemporary crises (Zaninovich, 1964). Our work on the 1962 Cuban crisis has revealed a startling (and, we feel, important) difference between the relationship of perception to behavior in the events of 1914 and 1962.

In 1914, perceptions -- particularly those of the leadership of the Dual Alliance -- were less than responsive to changes in behavior. One is tempted to speak of a "hostile set." This lack of fidelity seems to have led to a continual raising of the ante until it was too late to avoid the escalation of the Austro-Serbian War into a general European war. By contrast, in the Cuban crisis, the congruence between perception and behavior meant that non-hostile acts were seen as such and a mutual backdown from the crisis became possible (Holsti, et al., 1964). Explaining these two findings will keep us busy for some time to come.

One of the most hopeful signs in the development of the several approaches I have been outlining is the willingness of researchers who emphasize one approach to use other approaches. Karl Deutsch and

58

his associates, who have led in the development of aggregate data analysis, have also employed content analysis. Data from simulations have been produced by all the methods I have discussed, as well as more standardized techniques. Those of us who are currently emphasizing content analysis are also using aggregate data and doing secondary analysis of simulation data.

My purpose, in the presentation of this overview, is to try to communicate some of the excitement and ferment which characterizes the modern study of international politics. I have paid no attention to the disciplinary roots of the contributors to this revolution; psychologists have been -- and are -- full-time participants in these developments. To these individuals, those of us outside psychology owe a great deal, but we are also in the debt of the psychology profession in a larger sense: for a stimulating source of ideas, research findings, and social laws which will keep us busy doing research on their relevance to the international social context for years to come.

## Footnote

1. For Rummel's evaluation of the departure from linearity see Rummel, 1964, pp. 100-102.

## Bibliography

Brody, R. A., "Some Systematic Effects of the Spread of Nuclear Weapons Technology: A Study through Simulation of a Multi-Nuclear Future, " Journal of Conflict Resolution, 7 (1963), 663-753.

Crow, W. J., "A Study of Strategic Doctrines Using the Inter-Nation Simulation, " Journal of Conflict Resolution, 7 (1963), 580-89.

Crow, W. J. and L. N. Solomon, A Simulation Study of Strategic Doctrines, La Jolla, Calif.: Western Behavioral Sciences Institute, 1962.

Deutsch, K. W., Political Community at the International Level, Garden City, New York: Doubleday, 1954.

Deutsch, K. W., "Toward an Inventory of Basic Trends and Patterns in Comparative and International Politics, " American Political Science Review, 54 (1960), 34-57.

Deutsch, K. W., et al., Political Community in the North Atlantic Area, Princeton: Princeton University Press, 1956.

Guetzkow, H., C. Alger, R. Brody, R. Noel and R. C. Snyder, Simulation in International Relations: Developments for Research and Teaching, Englewood Cliffs, New Jersey: Prentice-Hall, 1963.

Hermann, C. and M. Hermann, Studies in Deterrence: Validation Studies of the Inter-Nation Simulation, China Lake, Calif.: USNOTS (NOTS TP3351), 1963.

Holsti, O., R. A. Brody and R. C. North, "Measuring Effect and Action in International Reaction Models: Empirical Materials from the 1962 Cuban Crisis, " (mimeo.) Stanford: Studies in International Conflict and Integration, 1964.

Holsti, O., R. Brody and R. C. North, Theory and Measurement of Interstate Relations: An Application of Automated Content Analysis, Stanford: Studies in International Conflict and Integration, 1964.

Holsti, O., R. A. Brody and R. C. North, "Violence and Hostility: The Path to World War, " (mimeo.) Stanford: Studies in International Conflict and Integration, 1964.

Jordan, N., "International Relations and the Psychologist, " Bulletin of the Atomic Scientists, 19 (Nov. 1963), 29-33.

Klineberg, O., The Human Dimension in International Relations, New York: Holt, Rinehart, Winston, 1964.

McClelland, C., "The Acute International Crisis, " World Politics, 14 (1961), 182-204.

McNeil, E. B., "International Relations and the Psychologist: The Scientific Gulf, " Bulletin of the Atomic Scientists, 19 (Nov., 1963), 33-35.

North, R. C., O. Holsti, M. G. Zaninovich and D. Zinnes, Content Analysis: A Handbook with Application for the Study of International Crisis, Evanston, Ill.: Northwestern University Press, 1963.

Osgood, C. E., "A Psychologist in International Affairs, " American Psychologist, 19 (1964), 111-118.

Osgood, C. E., G. J. Suci and P. H. Tannenbaum, The Measurement of Meaning, Urbana: University of Illinois Press, 1957.

Pruitt, D., "An Analysis of Responsiveness Between Nations, " Journal of Conflict Resolution, 6 (1962), 5-18.

Pruitt, D., Problem Solving in the Department of State, Denver: University of Denver Monograph Series in World Affairs, 1964-65.

Raser, J. R. and W. J. Crow, WINSAFE II: An Inter-Nation Simulation Study of Deterrence Postures Embodying Capacity to Delay Response, La Jolla, Calif.: Western Behavioral Sciences Institute, 1964.

Rummel, R., "Dimensions of Conflict Behavior Within and Between Nations, " General Systems, 8 (1963), 1-50.

Rummel, R., "Testing Some Possible Predictors of Conflict Within and Between Nations, " Peace Research Society (International), Papers, 1 (1964), 79-112.

Russett, B., Community and Contention, Cambridge: M. I. T. Press, 1963.

Sawyer, J., "How Can Psychology Contribute?" Bulletin of the Atomic Scientists, 19 (Nov., 1963), 35-38.

Snyder, R. C., "The Korean Decision (1950) and the Analysis of Crisis Decision-Making, " Working Group Reports, 1963 MORS Conference, 242-48.

Snyder, R. C., H. Bruck and B. Sapin, Foreign Policy Decision-Making, New York: Free Press of Glencoe, 1962.

Snyder, R. C. and G. Paige, "The United States Decision to Resist Aggression in Korea, " Administration Science Quarterly, 3 (1958), 341-78.

Whiting, A., China Crosses the Yalu, New York: Macmillan, 1960.

Wolfers, A., "The Actors in International Politics," in A. Wolfers, Discord and Collaboration, Baltimore: The Johns Hopkins University Press, 1962.

Zaninovich, M. G., An Operational Theory of Perceived Crisis, Ph. D. Dissertation, Stanford University, 1964.

Zetterberg, H., On Theory and Verification in Sociology, Rev. Ed., Totowa, N. J.: Bedminster Press, 1963.

Zinnes, D. A., R. C. North and H. E. Koch, Jr., "Capability, Threat, and the Outbreak of War," in J. N. Rosenau, International Politics and Foreign Policy, New York: Free Press of Glencoe, 1961, 469-82.

COMMITMENT TO PEACE WORK: A PRELIMINARY STUDY
OF DETERMINANTS AND SUSTAINERS OF BEHAVIOR CHANGE

Jerome D. Frank and Earl H. Nash
Johns Hopkins University

One effect of the huge destructive power of modern weapons has been to increase the number of active workers for peace. In all ages a few stalwart idealists have devoted their lives to this cause, but they characteristically have dissociated themselves from their society and its values and have sought to change human behavior by appeals to broad moral and religious principles, rather than to influence decision-makers or to affect specific policies. As a result, their efforts, though winning the admiration of some, have been scorned by most persons and have been essentially ineffective.

The new realities of modern weaponry have caused more and more people to recognize that war is ceasing to be a useful instrument in national policy and, in fact, threatens to put an end to mankind. This is leading to the emergence of new types of workers for enduring peace; they have a practical rather than an idealistic approach. They seek to influence policy-makers and to confine themselves to proposals within the possibility of fulfillment. The "peace movement" has become an aggregation of people covering a wide spectrum of attitudes, joined only by a concern for human survival. Their efforts may well be beginning to influence national policies.

It occurred to us that it might be interesting to make a survey of persons who have become active for peace in the recent past, since the experiences culminating in their new activities are still fresh in memory. Such a survey might be of considerable theoretical as well as practical interest. The experiences leading persons into peace activity represent an "experiment of nature," in Adolf Meyer's phrase, on determinants of change in attitudes and behavior. Since one of the determinants usually was an influencing person or group, it seemed worthwhile to consider the relevance of these experiences to other forms of interactions with an influencing agent, such as psychotherapy.

To limit our target population, we decided to confine our interest at first to persons who had become committed to peace activity as the result of a well defined, relatively brief experience that we have termed a "crucial episode." Though focus on such crucial episodes may exaggerate the apparent discontinuity in what usually is a gradual process, it has the potential advantage of highlighting determinants of

This study was supported in part by a grant from the U.S. Public Health Service. This aid is gratefully acknowledged.

Reprinted from the American Journal of Orthopsychiatry, 1965, 35, 106-119, with the permission of the authors and the American Orthopsychiatric Association.

attitude and behavior change that are ordinarily blurred.

Accordingly, we devised a detailed questionnaire for persons who had become active workers for peace as the result of a crucial episode in the recent past, defined simply as an identifiable time-limited experience that the subject could describe. After pre-testing and modification through interviews with volunteers made through personal contact, the questionnaire was sent to additional volunteers obtained the same way, or through an open letter printed in several peace and liberal publications. *

The questionnaire was organized in accordance with a suggestion of Kurt Lewin that change in social conduct involves a three-stage process: "unfreezing" of old patterns, changing them and "freezing" the changes. [9] The respondents first are asked to describe the crucial episode in their own terms. There follow four groups of questions. The first concerns the state of mind just preceding the episode. The second explores the episode itself. The third set of questions inquires into internal and environmental factors that sustain the new attitudes and behavior. A final set inquires about enduring personal qualities and aspects of background and life experience that may have predisposed the respondent to this type of experience. **

Most of the replies were immensely informative -- a tribute to the volunteers' perceptiveness, conscientiousness, verbal skill and willingness to reveal themselves. +

This report was based primarily on impressions gained from 92 respondents who had become active in working for peace since 1950. For 90 per cent the crucial episode had occurred since 1958. The respondents represented a very wide range of viewpoints, types of crucial episode and extent of change. They included persons who had become radical pacifists and those whose opposition to war was limited to the nuclear variety only. Some had experienced minimal change in attitude but had become more active in the service of views they always had held. At the other extreme, some had undergone changes as sweeping as those seen in religious conversions. For some the change occurred gradually as the result of prolonged reflection, reading and discussion. For others it occurred almost instantaneously. All, however, were able to single out a particular event as representing a definite step in their progress toward peace activity.

---

* The following journals published the letter: The Nation, The Progressive, Council for Correspondence Newsletter, SANE World, Turn Toward Peace mailing.

** This organization is based on the "situation analysis" found useful in studying phenomena of group psychotherapy. [12] These analyses centered on events that stood out from the ongoing flow of interactions. Phenomena related to these events were organized in terms of setting and effects.

+ We wish to express our deep appreciation to the participants in this study. We hope they will feel that the findings justify the time and effort they so freely gave.

The only feature that characterized virtually all volunteers --
indeed the criterion for sending them the questionnaire -- was an increase in activity for peace. Seventy-five per cent reported that the
increase was marked, and 24 per cent that it was moderate.

Identifying characteristics of the sample. Before proceeding
to the content of the replies, it may be well to report some of the
demographic characteristics of the sample. As might be expected
from the way it was obtained, it was not typical of the population at
large in some respects. Ninety-two per cent of the respondents had a
college or postgraduate education, and 51 per cent were students or
professionals -- that is, teachers, lawyers, physicians, writers or
artists. Twenty-three per cent were housewives. Seventeen per cent
(drawn about equally from professionals, students and housewives)
devoted most or all of their time to peace work.

About two-thirds were married, and one-tenth separated or
divorced. Most were in young or middle adulthood. Sixty-four per
cent were between 26 and 45. Only 5 per cent were over 55. Youth
was well represented; 20 per cent were under 25. Women preponder-
ated slightly over men (54 per cent to 46 per cent respectively).

One volunteer's experience. The following example of a definite crucial episode followed by considerable change in attitudes and
activities combines features found in most of the replies, and may
serve to introduce an analysis of them. *, **

> Two incidents occurred simultaneously in the fall of 1961
> that changed my life so completely I can hardly remember
> what I was like before then!
>
> When the Soviets resumed testing and tensions had
> mounted over the wall, nuclear war for the first time seemed
> imminently possible. I very rationally decided to put into
> action the vague "defense plans" I'd reserved for such an
> emergency. It was simple. We'd build a fallout shelter in
> our basement, stock it with food and be the first in our neigh-
> borhood to survive an atomic attack. So I sent for govern-
> ment pamphlets and began to read. Suddenly it dawned on me
> that they were talking about protection from 15 megatons, not
> 50 megatons and, at that, they were making no promises. It
> had honestly never dawned on me that there was no place to
> hide. I've never known such panic and chilling, paralyzing
> fear and profound depression.
>
> Soon thereafter I received a call from a longtime peace
> worker about whom I'd heard much but whom I'd never met.
> She said she was putting a letter in the paper inviting women
> who were deeply concerned about the dangerous drift in affairs
> to stand in silent vigil in front of the county courthouse at noon

---

* In all quotations details have been changed to conceal the respondent's identity.

** Italics are the authors'.

on November 1. I was tremendously impressed by the things she had to say about the responsibility of individual citizens. She said she wanted the names of new people to appear in the paper, and because of my involvement with the local international club, she'd called on me. I said I wouldn't be caught dead standing on a corner like that; that I thought demonstrations did more harm than good because people figured you were exhibitionists or beatniks and paid no attention to what you were saying. However, I did express my deep fears and concern and said I'd be willing to invite some neighbors in for coffee at the noon hour to discuss ways in which we might be able as individuals to reverse the trends toward war. The peace worker asked me to append such an invitation to her original letter for other women who felt they couldn't stand on a street corner. This I was willing to do and signed the letter. My name appeared first in the listing of some 10 women who signed the public letter, so maybe this is why I received so many phone calls from perfect strangers. All of a sudden life was different. There were other women who felt as I did; we had found each other and out of our fears came a new determination to influence the decisions that suddenly seemed to have such a direct and threatening relationship to our lives.

From this letter, these phone calls and demonstration (which I did not attend) came the nucleus of our local Women for Peace. It might interest you to know that yours truly was in charge of the next demonstration at the county courthouse. It became apparent to me that some things can only be said in this way -- extraordinary events call for extraordinary actions -- and the amazing thing was that the esprit we'd developed among ourselves made being part of a public spectacle an uplifting experience.

Preceding the crucial episode she had avoided thinking about nuclear war and trusted for protection to government policies: "I remember feeling a certain confidence in SAC and the DEW line preparations. I felt a certain security in the arms build-up. "

Following these events the respondent solidified her commitment by becoming editor of the local monthly bulletin of Women Strike for Peace. She also continued to write to government officials, fill speaking engagements and participate in demonstrations. She added liberal and pacifist literature to her reading and joined Women Strike for Peace, CORE and NAACP.

She came to regard nuclear war as a greater danger than communism in contrast to her view before the crucial episode. Her increased concern with peace generalized to related attitudes: ". . . now I see a deeper and more imperative relationship between civil rights and the arms race -- and hunger in undeveloped countries and problems of world peace. The solution to these problems now seems inextricably tied to the problems of nuclear arms. "

She gives as the main sustainers of her new attitudes the convic-

tion of the rightness and the importance of her activities, new information, the support of other persons and membership in new groups. She
feels that she has been moderately effective and that her activities have
alleviated unpleasant feelings about nuclear arms, enhanced her self-
esteem and reduced her self-doubts.

The ground may have been laid for the crucial episode by attendance at a Quaker college many years before and "personal abhorrence
of all forms of violence. "

In summary, the crucial episode for this respondent combined a
news event and the influence of a person. The former sharply heightened her perception of the danger of nuclear war and impelled her to
try to cope with it. When she realized the futility of her plan of action,
she became acutely anxious. This may have increased her receptivity
to a peace worker who suggested another course of action involving
public commitment. This action revealed unsuspected, strong group
support for a variety of peace activities. This reinforced her new
viewpoint and heightened her sense of effectiveness. Concomitantly
with her new activities, she exposed herself to new information, her
attitudes to other issues related to peace became more salient, her
self-doubts decreased and her self-esteem increased, reinforcing her
changed outlook and behavior. In the background was an abhorrence of
violence (not reflected in her dominant attitude just before the crucial
episode).

Let us now turn to a systematic review of the replies with special reference to personality characteristics of the respondents, experiences sensitizing them to the crucial episode, prodromal attitudes,
aspects of the crucial episode itself, and, finally, factors which sustained or discouraged the changes in viewpoint and behavior following
it.

Personality and background characteristics of the respondents.
The respondents for the most part were stable, capable and productive
citizens, active in issues concerned with human welfare, liberal politically (73 per cent) and international minded (68 per cent). Thirty-
seven per cent gave no religious affiliation, and 30 per cent were Uni-
tarians or Quakers. Seventy-four per cent stated that they were moderately or very dissatisfied with things as they were. Nonconformity
with the dominant social environment was mirrored by internal conflicts. Fifty-three per cent were bothered by self-doubts; 52 per cent
had changed their religious faiths; and 40 per cent had undergone psychotherapy before or after the crucial episode. (The last group were
probably highly over-represented since they knew the request to fill out
the questionnaire came from a psychiatrist. ) The following quotations
are illustrative?

I find it difficult to say I (or anyone) was ever completely
typical of anything.

I have never been unquestioning about the status quo ...
early I found myself in tune with those who explored and
worked for change.

66

I am a person who has spent most of her life making niches for herself, usually in localities nobody else cared for, and working in them until she compelled others to praise her for her efforts.

I have been prone to self-doubts and dissatisfactions ... I wonder if I'm looking for a reason to vent this particular kind of anger. I'm satisfied that the motivation is real, but I react because of childhood experiences to arbitrary acts; patronizing attitudes, and "leave it to us, " hypercritical authority.

These attitudes were related to characteristics of the family of origin. Seventy-six per cent of the respondents described their families as not completely typical of the surrounding community, and the parents of 53 per cent differed from each other in political affiliation, religion, or number of generations in the United States:

I was brought up as the only Protestant, English family in an Irish town. Traitors in school were heroes at home and vice versa. It gives one a healthy attitude of scepticism. Father was in the British army and made it all very glamorous. Mother would ask gentle questions, such as "Did the Malayans really want you there?" The conflict between my parents made me ready.

This type of background may be related to the fact that 49 per cent described themselves as "non-joiners, " but it was also consistent with the equally common pattern of allegiance to non-conforming groups or causes.

As a child I identified with the newcomer, the oddball (but) I very definitely did* belong to a community of non-conformists ... my parents were part of this community and so were my school friends ... I did not feel alone against the world ... I knew where I fitted in very well, so much so that I never had an undue need to "conform" or to "join. "

Sensitizing experiences. Against this background, some respondents felt that they had been especially sensitized to the crucial episode by certain life experiences. A small minority reported firsthand or vicarious experience with the horrors of war. Others reported special experiences that made the implications of nuclear weapons personally real to them. A mother whose daughter was severely burned wrote:

The pain and agony that she visibly went through made me realize the horror of Hiroshima and Nagasaki. I felt what all

---

* Italics in this and all following quotations are the respondents'.

67

those other mothers must have felt to see their children
burned and dying . . . I did not find an outlet for the intense
feelings this accident gave me until the Soviets started testing
about a year later.

The same event struck home to a lady recovering from an operation for cancer:

I remember thinking now I'll never get well . . . It occurred to me that . . . cancer can be induced by man-made
chemicals and that people need to be awakened to that. I
should really do my best to do as much as I could. It was a
decision which came while I was standing in the bedroom --
it seems vivid -- and it was definite. I was surprised at my
own firmness.

Indirectly sensitizing experiences were sojourns in foreign countries and planned or recent moves that helped to detach the respondent
from his former reference groups:

I had just returned from a year in Africa . . . (which) . . .
increased my sensitivity and receptiveness to new experiences
and caused me to think along lines previously ignored.

Our intense concern about this issue is related, in retro-
spect, to several concurrent personal life problems. My wife
and I were terminating our analyses and preparing for an
eventual move east. These events were extremely stressful
for us both, and, in some respects, had qualities of "catastrophe" that the imminent threat of nuclear war fitted in with
quite closely.

The morals and the ethics of the people (in our new neigh-
borhood) seemed "new" and different. People talked and acted
like lunatics. For two months I began to fear for my sanity.
Finally I asked my husband. When he said "they're the ones
that are crazy," I was relieved.

Other personal experiences that weakened the respondent's at-
tachment to his customary reference groups included divorce, deaths
in the immediate family and psychotherapy.

Being an adolescent can be seen as a similar sensitizing experience. The adolescent is a "marginal man,"[8] losing contact with the
reference groups of childhood and not yet committed to the values and
viewpoints of adults. In the process of forming his adult identity, he
is especially open to new influences, especially those which offer him
a strong self-consistent value system. In addition, his struggle to
free himself from parental controls draws him to minority causes. In
our sample, the adolescents showed the most sweeping changes in activities and attitudes. Some had started to swing back from their new
position, and others may do so. For this age group, the influencing

agent was always a person or group that seemed to dramatize both rebellion and idealism.

One came under the influence of "a socialist . . . extremely bitter -- a fascinating speaker . . . (who) . . . showed my
(militaristic, conservative) attitude to be bourgeois, emotionally conformist and reactionary, and demonstrated the hypoc-
risy of my former idols." Another visited a Quaker camp.
Up to that time "I had never thought that there was an alternative to defending freedom through violent means . . . I asked
myself what I was doing in life and what the world really was
about . . . Within the space of two weeks I literally became a
peace 'fanatic.' I needed something to latch onto."

Prodromal attitudes. One may surmise that all respondents
felt somewhat conflicted about the issues posed by nuclear weapons.
Some were aware of their conflict. Others resolved or escaped from
it by avoiding the question or relying on the government to solve it.

Examples of the last two attitudes are: "I was only
slightly concerned because I knew little about nuclear arms
and just as little about politics. It was a great big problem
but one far away from me." "I felt that whatever the U.S.
policy was, it was right and I needn't question it."
An example of conscious conflict is: "The build-up
seemed frighteningly dangerous. Disarmament, which I had
not really followed year by year, seemed hopeless. I dis-
trusted the cold-war caricatures of the Russian government
and was worried and angered by our own diplomacy and press
-- without really having a clear view of constructive policy.
I did not accept the notion that we really had to fight the Russians at every turn . . . I thought that if we could become less
combative, they also could be, but I wasn't sure."

The most common attitude prior to the crucial episode is well
described in the following passage: sympathy with disarmament coupled with a feeling of helplessness that paralyzed action:

I had a general predisposition to pacifism and to distrust in the establishment (but it was pretty vague and very
ineffectual) . . . I shared the preconceived idea with most
people . . . that political matters are a kind of fatalistically
determined thing which the individual can't do anything about.
I knew better but emotionally I had not been aroused to combat the inertia. It was as though (my convictions) were already piling up and ready for someone to wake them into
action, like a bonfire ready to be lit.

The crucial episode -- environmental components. The crucial
episode that "lit the bonfire" can be viewed from the standpoints of the

respondent and his environment. The latter almost always contained a person or group that acted as advocates or representatives of the new approach, or both. They functioned partly as models, demonstrating a course of action the respondent could follow, and as persuaders, convincing him by logic and new information. [6] In our sample the most frequent influencers were groups demonstrating for peace -- especially those on November 1, 1961, organized by Women Strike for Peace -- and individual peace workers, including public figures, colleagues or friends of the respondent. Usually the contact with the influencing agent was personal and direct, but for some respondents it was mediated by the printed page.

Sometimes the crucial episode also included an event that broke through the respondent's protective apathy and increased his receptivity to the person. Occasionally the reverse occurred; exposure to a person prepared the respondent to be activated by an event. About one-third of the respondents (37 per cent) were activated in 1961, the year of the Berlin wall, Russian resumption of testing and the public controversy over private fallout shelters. One, two, or all of these made the dangers of nuclear war personally real, confronted the respondent with the responsibility of making a decision (to build or not to build a shelter) and exposed the inadequacy of his means for seeking safety, as in the first example cited above.

The crucial episode -- personal reactions and behavioral responses. The reactions of the respondents may be divided for convenience into emotional, cognitive and behavioral.

The most common emotions were fear and anger. They often were remarkably intense, giving substance to the simile of the bonfire. Ninety-six per cent scored their emotional reactions as moderately or very strong, and 60 per cent used the latter category, which was the extreme of the scale. Examples of the most intense reactions are:

> The fear was monumental . . . I thought I had gone crazy.

> I felt completely disoriented. I would literally shiver from nervousness and fear and had very frequent crying spells . . . I hung onto words I had heard or read which seemed to bear some ray of hope and sanity.

> My "conversion" had to do with the shattering of my sense of security as an American. I suddenly felt totally vulnerable, horrified and amazed that no one else seemed in the slightest aware or concerned that we were all probably going to be annihilated.

Like fear, anger often was very strong. The respondents used words like "outrage," "furious," "incensed," "damned annoyed" to describe the feeling, which was directed either against the country's leadership, or against groups whom they had mistakenly expected to be promoting disarmament. It may be that the discovery that those whom one counted on as allies were really in the enemy camp would be especially conflict-producing, as in the following:

> I hadn't really felt that top people in government and the army themselves really believed what they said publicly. I thought intelligent people such as my scientist friends saw things as I did. When I found they didn't, I was shocked into action.

> I am surprised by the absence of moral standards in those professing to be Christians. Brotherhood is apparently something one believes but never practices. The clergy, the scientists, the press have failed the public.

> The fact that some clergy of all faiths could be found to sanction inhuman behavior such as using a gun against one's neighbor to keep him out of your shelter had a profound effect on me ... Was, in fact, this kind of society worth saving?

Not all emotional reactions were unpleasant. Eighteen per cent also experienced exhilaration or relief at having found a resolution of their dilemma. Those who responded favorably to an influencing agent often described him in glowing terms, implying considerable emotion. Twenty-six per cent reported both negative and positive emotions.

Of some theoretical interest is the fact that some of the respondents who were most influenced had conflicting feelings toward the person or group advocating action for peace, as the following quotations suggest:

> Our small group had reservations about the qualities of the (peace) demonstrators that we later identified as brittle, militant postures which weren't at all feminine ...

> For a few days I eyed all "these pacifists" with a jaundiced eye, because the thought of anything opposing the "road to freedom" and our government seemed un-American.

A man and his wife had a very mixed reaction to a Quaker study institute they attended:

> They said that problems of the world were related to us, that we were at fault. I remember getting up and shouting at a man who said we need some "rectification" like the Chinese. We could not accept that our government was to blame hence could not accept protest against authority as relevant action, but no other was clear.

> I went back as a leader the next year. Then we were clear we were angry at them, spent a lot of energy fighting them. They tended to cry alarm, then pooh-poohed various concrete courses of action because they did not get at the Pentagon, etc. ... The leading advocate of non-violence was coercive in leading the meeting.

This stimulated a tremendous conflict. Peace work became a kind of working through the insoluble dilemma they posed.

The most characteristic cognitive responses to the crucial episode were a changed perception of the problem (80 per cent), often coupled with a need for more information (47 per cent) and a heightened sense of personal responsibility. These usually were accompanied by a new sense that one could do something as an individual. These related themes are expressed in the following passages:

I saw that a problem those around me avoided could at least be approached.

(The crucial episode) changed my preconceived idea that I was not responsible for the betterment of conditions, that I was powerless to change things ... realization of personal responsibility and the necessity of rebellion.

The degree of danger and the quality of responses to it made me feel that one no longer could depend on officials of the governments concerned to remove the threat of nuclear war ... and that I must assume responsibility as an individual -- continuous and direct responsibility, if the threat were to be met with effective response.

Finally, the crucial episode may be viewed from the standpoint of the respondents' actions. Two features were striking. The first was initiative. Some respondents were mobilized by an event to which they were passively exposed, such as a news item, but the great majority were showing some initiative at the time, if only talking with neighbors about building a fallout shelter, going to a lecture or reading a book. The second feature of the respondent's action was public commitment, sometimes preceded by a brief period of bewilderment or uncertainty as to what to do. The act of commitment might be writing a letter to the paper or to a senator, participating in a demonstration or organizing a meeting.

The crucial episode -- determinants of duration of effects. Ninety-five per cent of the crucial episodes had occurred at least two years previously (only 5 per cent occurred in 1963), and most respondents had maintained the changed pattern of activities. In this connection, a reminder is in order that the sample was self-selected. This precludes any conclusions as to the proportion of persons who are changed permanently by a crucial episode. Those who experienced only a transient effect might well have been less inclined to volunteer to fill out the questionnaire than those who were still active.

The most characteristic pattern was some months of very intense and often diffuse activity, falling off to a pattern that could be sustained. As one respondent put it:

My activities have spread out for the long haul. I've dropped the crisis flavor.

For the few who have ceased, or virtually so, one reason given was completion of the task initially set, as in the lady who determined to recruit members for a particular peace organization, and stopped after she had run through all her friends and acquaintances. Others stopped because of external pressures or, more rarely, being too emotionally aroused by concentrating on the peace issue.

A unique combination of unbearable external and internal pressures may be illustrated by the following:

> All my friends are gone and I've been isolated. I was faced with divorce from my wife ... (who) ... threatened suicide if I continued to incur the wrath of the radical right. I lost my job ...
>
> The confusion became very great and finally I sought psychotherapy ... to calm me down and give me an opportunity to clarify the situation for myself and build back my self-esteem.

For those who continued to be active, the chief intrapersonal sustainers were conviction of the rightness of their actions (98 per cent); heightened self-esteem (79 per cent), and a reduction of unpleasant feelings, such as anxiety and depression (72 per cent).

In all instances the new attitudes toward nuclear war were anchored by similar attitudes toward related issues. That is, they were congruent with a more comprehensive belief system. [13] Eighty-six per cent reported that their involvement in peace activity led to an increased concern with race relations, poverty, overpopulation and other issues of human welfare. The remaining 14 per cent reported that they were involved in such issues before starting peace activity. The most sweeping statement of generalization of concern was:

> I could no longer avoid relating almost every aspect of my life (certainly the most important -- profession, home, religion, ethics) to the reality of nuclear age problems.

Further evidence of striving to make one's belief systems consistent is that 92 per cent of the respondents regarded nuclear armaments as a greater threat than communism, but 51 per cent came to this view only after they had become peace activists.* This shift in viewpoint is an illustration of the tendency to reduce "cognitive dissonance."[3] Support of nuclear disarmament would be inconsistent with a view that communism was the greater danger, creating an internal conflict. An effective way of resolving this dilemma was to decide that nuclear armaments were the greater relative threat, by upgrading one's fear of them or downgrading the fear of communism, and this is

---

* Of the remainder, 5 per cent either failed to answer the question or scored both threats as equal, leaving only 3 per cent who scored communism as the greater threat after the crucial episode.

what the respondents did.*

With respect to the environment, respondents reinforced their new position by reading more "peace" literature. Ninety-two per cent listed new information as an important sustainer of their activities. They proselytized among their friends and maintained their public commitment by continuing to participate in demonstrations, writing public letters and the like. They sought new like-minded friends and groups. Seventy-nine per cent reported that some or all of their friends were different, and 91 per cent that their participation in peace groups had moderately or markedly increased.

> As a result of my experience I had to seek out the peacemakers -- they are the real people I spent nearly 40 years of my life without knowing.

Finally, support of family members was important to many:

> If my wife and I had not repeatedly and extensively discussed our views, fears, plans, feelings, neither of us would have done as much or learned as much ... as we have. In fact, these issues have been crucial to the deepening of our own relationship and led us to a more satisfactory balance of our philosophies of life.

## Discussion

In attempting to interpret these preliminary findings, certain cautions must be kept in mind. The sample is heterogeneous in many ways, so that any generalizations would be unlikely to apply to more than a part of it. Internal analyses of the replies now under way, comparing different sub-groups of the sample and relations between items, should yield a firmer basis for inference.

Another ground for caution is the self-selection of the respondents, which makes all conclusions highly tentative in the absence of controls. Ideally findings should be checked against those from matched subjects who had not become peace activists and another matched group actively campaigning for a "forward strategy" based on relentless confrontation of the Communists with superior military force.[15] Truly adequate controls may be difficult to obtain, but we plan to explore the possibilities.

Before considering the results themselves, attention should be called to two features of the context of peace activity today. The first is the changed nature of modern warfare. Its massive, impersonal

---

* This finding is consistent with a public opinion survey that found the best single predictor of support for aggressive cold war policies was the person's attitude toward the Soviet Union. If he feared it, he supported aggressive policies even if he realized that nuclear war meant the end of our civilization.[10]

destructiveness jeopardizes not only individual human lives but the structure of civilization itself and the future of mankind. [11] As a result, the struggle against war has enlisted the efforts not only of those who seek personal survival, but those who are concerned about mankind's future. Furthermore, in contrast to the past, war is no longer a possible way of defending the democratic values of individual worth and human dignity, so rejection of war and the search for more workable methods of resolving conflict have a new pertinence.

An additional relevant point may be that today no value system seems clearly to dominate American life. Many ideologies and groups are competing for the allegiance of its citizens. In the past most workers for peace were clearly in a protesting minority against a dominant value system. Today this is not so clear. Although some peace groups still see themselves as in sharp opposition to society, others find themselves able to work within the power structure.

Against this context, the backgrounds and personality characteristics of certain of the respondents may be relevant to their peace activities. In general, they see themselves not as opposed to American society but as trying to preserve it, and resemble their neighbors in their family, social and work patterns. Three features seem to characterize most of them: a high degree of initiative, a lively concern for human welfare and independence of thought. In combination, these qualities may have heightened their awareness of the threat to human welfare posed by modern weapons, made them less willing to accept uncritically the official policies for coping with it and more inclined to act on their own understanding of the problem. Thus they became active following a more or less sudden subjective conviction that generally accepted national policies were jeopardizing human survival.

Their capacity to detach themselves from the views of the surrounding community may be related to the fact that their "assumptive world"[2, 5] was formed in a family that was not entirely harmonious with its surroundings or was inwardly conflicted, or both. Exposed to various viewpoints from the start, they probably are not firmly committed to any particular belief system, and hence can shift more easily from one to another than persons brought up in a more homogeneous environment. This intellectual independence may have enabled them to make a more correct appraisal than their more conformist neighbors of the peril facing man. Their rejection of the dominant viewpoint for a more unpopular one would then represent no more than abandonment of a position they perceived as erroneous for a more appropriate one.

More complex motivations, however, are evident in some respondents, perhaps also traceable to the family backgrounds. Family conflicts may be reflected in inner conflicts, manifested by self-doubts and dissatisfactions. Some may have failed to develop an adequate sense of identity and may hope to achieve it by adherence to groups with a strong, self-consistent ideology.

A childhood containing sources of conflict and tension might also heighten a person's sensitivity to environmental threats and make him especially attuned to the unpleasant features of conflict.

Thus peace activity could serve many psychological functions. It might be a working toward a world that contains fewer sources of threat or a reaction formation enabling the participants to conceal their anger from themselves. Antagonism to aggressive groups in our society, such as "militarists," may sometimes be an expression of heightened sensitivity to attributes of others that one dislikes in oneself. [7] Peace activities, by offering a socially approved way of expressing angry feelings, also may be viewed as a form of "pro-social acting out" -- a channeling of destructive feelings into constructive activity. [4]

These covert motivations operate in everyone. There is no reason to think that they are more prevalent in our respondents than in any group or segment of society.

The crucial episode itself, as well as its prodromes and aftermaths, highlights certain general aspects of attitude and behavior change. Preceding the crucial episode, many respondents were in a state of uncertainty, and some had undergone experiences that specifically heightened their sensitivity to nuclear arms. That is, their response patterns had become "unfrozen."

The actual change was precipitated by events that further heightened their tension. Three related factors can be distinguished in these occurrences. One is a heightening of the threat of nuclear destruction which became personally real. A second is the discovery that those they had relied on to fight for disarmament would not do so and that the suggested means of protection would be inadequate. These led to emotional responses, the frequency and intensity of which were striking. This may be partly a reflection of the criterion for inclusion, which was that the subjects must have undergone a change of attitudes or behavior in a relatively short time. Arousal of affect accompanies all personality change, but it might be expected to be stronger when the change is abrupt than when it is gradual.

The third factor was the arousal of a feeling of personal responsibility for doing something to remove the danger. In keeping with their active orientation toward life, the respondents did not wait passively for someone to show them a solution but actively sought guidance by reading, going to a lecture, participating in a demonstration, or talking with a friend. The fact that the initiative came from them may have increased their receptivity.

Changes in viewpoint and behavior following the crucial episode were intrapsychically sustained by a sense of righteousness accompanied by heightened self-esteem. Internal conflict was reduced by changes in other belief systems that reinforced the new viewpoint.

With respect to the environment, support by members of the immediate family seemed to reinforce the new behavior, just as their opposition might be discouraging. With characteristic initiative, the respondents bolstered their new patterns by seeking new confirmatory information, by making new friends, by joining new sympathetic groups and by efforts to convince others privately and publicly. Public commitment to the new view may have helped to sustain it, in accordance with the experimental finding that opinions which people make known to others are harder to change than privately held ones. [1] In this connec-

tion, contrary to oft-expressed views as to their futility, public demonstrations converted many passive sympathizers into active ones. Two
features may be responsible for their effectiveness. They aroused a
strong feeling of group solidarity, and participation represented a public commitment, from which it was hard to retreat.

Certain aspects of the crucial episodes seem relevant to psychotherapy. That similar processes may be involved is suggested by
the fact that some respondents resemble favorable candidates for psychotherapy in many ways. They are prone to self-doubts, dissatisfac-
tion and inner conflicts. In addition, they are well educated, verbally
adept, emotionally responsive and aware of and willing to reveal their
inner feelings. This is reflected in the informativeness and perceptiveness of many replies to the questionnaire.

They also resembled good psychotherapeutic candidates in that
they assumed personal responsibility for solving their dilemmas and
actively sought help from a person or group.

Theories of psychotherapy stress the significance of emotional
interplay between patient and therapist. Similarly, the influencing
agent for peace activity characteristically elicited a strong emotional
response. The feelings he aroused usually were favorable, but sometimes they were mixed. An admixture of negative feelings did not
necessarily reduce his influence. This is consistent with the observation that angry feelings toward a psychotherapist, whether or not based
on negative transference, need not hamper therapy and may indeed contribute to its success. It also accords with animal studies showing that
any strong emotion heightens social bonds. [14]

The influencing agent was not only a stimulator of emotion but,
to varying degrees, a model with whom the respondent could identify
and a source of new information and logical argument. Psychothera-
pists have analogous functions. The findings of the questionnaire suggest that the purely cognitive and rational aspects of psychotherapy
often may be more important than is generally recognized.

Although many types of psychotherapy seek to produce attitude
and personality change, these have been notoriously difficult to demonstrate objectively. All forms of psychotherapy, however, if successful, produce changes in patients' social behavior. These, in turn,
elicit new reinforcing responses from other persons that strengthen
the new patterns. The respondents' efforts to find individual and group
support for their new activities support the view that this may be an
important aspect of the psychotherapeutic process as well.

With few exceptions, changes in behavior far exceeded changes
in attitude. The latter occurred almost exclusively in adolescents,
whose identities were not yet crystallized. The crucial episode typically served chiefly to clarify existing attitudes, to make them more
salient or to remove blocks to acting on them such as feelings of fatal-
ism or impotence. This is an encouraging reminder that changes in
behavior resulting from psychotherapy may be extensive and have
wide social and personal repercussions, even without much change in
underlying attitudes or basic personality structure. In any case,
most of the questionnaire replies are consistent with the impression

gained from psychotherapy that genuine attitude change usually takes time. When it appears to be produced abruptly, this is probably because the apparent agent of change "lit the bonfire" that already was laid.

Summary

This is a preliminary analysis of 92 replies to a questionnaire filled out by volunteers who had become active in peace work as the result of a crucial episode in the recent past. The major categories of findings are predisposing personal and environmental factors; emotional, cognitive and behavioral features of the episode itself, and intrapersonal and interpersonal sustainers of changes following it. The findings are discussed in terms of their relevance to determinants of attitude and behavior change, including psychotherapy.

References

1. Abelson, H. I. 1959. Persuasion. Springer. New York, N. Y.: pp. 31-34.
2. Cantril, H. 1950. The "Why" of Man's Experience. MacMillan. New York, N. Y.
3. Festinger, L. 1957. A Theory of Cognitive Dissonance. Row, Peterson & Co., Evanston, Ill.
4. Fishman, J. R. and F. Solomon. 1962. Psychological observations on the student sit-in movement. In Proceedings of the Third World Congress of Psychiatry. University of Toronto Press. Toronto, Canada: pp. 1133-1138.
5. Frank, J. D. 1961. Persuasion and Healing: A Comparative Study of Psychotheraphy. Johns Hopkins Press. Baltimore, Md.
6. Kelman, H. C. 1963. The role of the group in the induction of therapeutic change. Int. Jour. Group Psychother. 13(4): 399-432.
7. Laughlin, H. P. 1954. King David's anger. Psychoanal. Quart. 23(1): 87-95.
8. Lewin, K. 1951. Field Theory in Social Science. Harper. New York, N. Y.: pp. 141-145.
9. Lewin, K. 1958. Group decision and social change. In Readings in Social Psychology. E. E. Maccoby, T. M. Newcomb, and E. L. Hartley, Eds. Holt, Rinehart and Winston. New York, N. Y.: 210f.
10. Modigliani, A. 1963. The public and the cold war. War/Peace Report. 3: 7-9.
11. Morgenthau, H. J. 1961. Death in the nuclear age. Commentary. 32(3): 231-234.
12. Powdermaker, F. and J. D. Frank. 1953. Group Psychotherapy: Studies in Methodology of Research and Therapy. Harvard University Press. Cambridge, Mass.

13. Rokeach, M. 1960. The Open and Closed Mind. Basic Books, Inc. New York, N. Y.
14. Scott, J. P. 1962. Critical periods in behavioral development. Science. 138:949-958.
15. Strausz-Hupé, R., W. R. Kintner and S. T. Possony. 1961. A Forward Strategy for America. Harpers. New York, N. Y.

# PSYCHOLOGY, PSYCHOLOGISTS, AND DISARMAMENT

Thomas S. Lough
United States Arms Control and Disarmament Agency

I am going to talk about two things today. First I am going to suggest some psychological principles which psychologists might find useful in trying to communicate their findings to policymakers. Secondly I am going to urge that more psychologists become involved in studying and solving current social problems.

Because certain portions of what I am about to say may seem unduly critical of psychology, let me begin with the partial disclaimer that any criticisms I have of our field can in general be levelled at other fields -- and not even only at the behavioral sciences -- with equal justification. Or, you and our discussant may decide, with equal lack of justification.

I might also add that as a psychologist, addressing a group of psychologists, I feel more comfortable, being critical, than I would if I were simply an otherwise unidentified member of the U. S. Arms Control and Disarmament Agency addressing, say, a group of political scientists or Chinese experts. You people can always respond to criticism by a fellow psychologist by suggesting that I am really just working out certain problems with authority, or by pointing out that I never did have a very full grasp of the field, or something along those lines.

On to the psychology of psychologists and disarmament. Let me first make two assumptions: one, that psychologists who are interested in disarmament generally are in favor of some rational approach to solving the arms problem, and they feel research or analysis of some kind will be helpful in achieving these solutions. In other words, they are not just interested in arms control and disarmament discussions, negotiations and theories as contemporary phenomena like Beatle-mania and women's fashions; rather they are interested in doing something about weapons of mass destruction. And being rational scientists, our credo is that facts and reason will enable us better to cope with the problem of such weapons than in the absence of facts and reason. This is to say that I assume those of us who are interested in disarmament, in a professional sense, are interested in doing applied research on the subject.

The second assumption is that applied research on this subject is not different from applied research on any other subject, in that you want to understand the problem and then communicate your understanding to those who are in a position to solve it. You want your knowledge

This paper is based on a talk delivered at the Georgetown University Symposium on Psychology and International Relations on June 27, 1964. The views herein expressed are those of the author and do not necessarily represent the views of any agency of the United States Government.

and insights to be taken into account by people who have the power to make decisions.

Parenthetically, I understand that it is also possible to become personally influential -- to become a decisionmaker. I am obviously not the one to tell you how to become influential in the area of disarmament.

But I do want to point out that we psychologists do know something about how to communicate with other people, including people who make decisions, and that we might want to use this knowledge in communicating the results of our applied research on arms control and disarmament.

First, we know that information is most readily accepted if it fits into the frame of reference of the receiver of the information. This means we should try to see the world as the receiver sees it -- to put ourselves in his shoes. If the language, style, evidence, or assumptions are too different from what he is used to, the message will not be understood or accepted. Taking as an example the kind of message that might be understood and accepted by a typical State Department officer: It should be written in a language he understands; it must make explicit or implicit reference to accepted U.S. policy objectives; and it must include arguments and evidence with which he is familiar.

On the matter of language, I have yet to find a social science idea which cannot be translated into English. To be sure, you often lose some of the precision you want to keep when you are communicating with fellow social scientists, but this is to be expected. This is a problem for all special fields. However, sometimes you may be surprised at what comes out when you translate into English, too. Sometimes a major area of inquiry, such as cognitive dissonance, or frustration and aggression, sounds rather trivial or self-evident when described in English. A not uncommon response by a layman is "Do you need to study that?" The answer, of course, is "Yes, if we are to understand this phenomenon." But, as I will suggest in a minute, it may be true that too much of psychology is devoted to questions which are self-evident or trivial to the non-psychologist.

Before I leave this matter of language, I should add that the person in government uses language in special ways. Although people in the non-military and non-technical branches of government do not use any strange words, they do attach precise meanings to certain words, that sometimes the person outside government is not aware of. Words like treaty, agreement, understanding, negotiation, discussion, conference, committee, group, formal, informal, and consultation, have precise meanings for a man on the political side of government. Another thing: because written agreements, announcements and treaties are often written to be intentionally vague on some points and precise on others, a political officer is very sensitive to the use and non-use of qualifying language. For a trivial example, the word government means all branches of government, including state, federal and local, executive, judicial and legislative. The more specific you can be, the better he will understand, the better he will think you understand, and the more you will in fact understand.

I also mentioned that in communicating with the people on the political side of the executive branch of government you should make explicit or implicit reference to accepted U.S. policy objectives, such as NATO; an Atlantic trade community; a political unification in Europe within which the reunification of Germany may take place; establishing a more reasonable relationship with the USSR; strengthening our relationship with countries in the Southern hemisphere; achieving stability in underdeveloped countries, including assisting them in developing stable political and economic systems; containing the spread of Communism; encouraging the self-determination of nations now under communist rule; and achieving military stability in Europe.

This does not mean you cannot be critical of some of these objectives, or that you cannot point out possible inconsistencies among them, or better ways of pursuing certain of them. But it does mean you should be familiar with these objectives, know the accepted arguments that support them, and the standard arguments that are used to defeat challenges to them.

This brings me to the question of evidence. The policy decision-maker is used to dealing with history. He makes history, as we usually use the term, and he believes in it. Evidence, for him, are statements by political leaders, the facts of various wars, agreements and treaties, and of course the intelligence estimates of military, economic, and political capabilities and intentions of other nations. I am convinced that it is very difficult to get him to accept as important evidence any of the data with which we as psychologists are used to dealing. He certainly does not see psychological data as providing a sound basis for policy decisions. And if you will put yourself in his shoes, I think you will understand his view.

So where does this leave us? Given what I believe is the sound psychological principle that information is most readily accepted if it fits into the frame of reference of the receiver, is there any hope of the psychologist rephrasing his knowledge so that it fits into the political decisionmaker's framework? I think so, but I think it will take some doing. (Parenthetically, we might ask why the policymaker does not instead frame his questions in psychological terms. I think the answer is that he has little time or inclination to do this. For better or worse he is the policymaker, and it is we who are trying to serve him, rather than the reverse.)

A second psychological principle we might use in trying to communicate with a policyplanner or decisionmaker is that information is accepted as a function of the credibility and status of the speaker. In practical terms, this means that being a psychologist is not necessarily a bonus in reaching and communicating with a policymaker; your best bet is to be someone who has a reputation -- or at least claims expertise as -- either a specialist in a particular applied problem area which is of some interest to the policymaker, or as an acute observer of people and society. I am saying that as simply psychologists, we are not necessarily credible sources, although some psychologists have reputations which give them status as thinkers about policy problems. I should add, of course, that psychology is not the only field which has trouble being seen as a high-status, highly credible source.

Finally, we have the psychological principle about opportunity for exposure. It has become a truism that the policymaker has already too much to read. Beyond what he must read, he will usually read that which he feels is relevant. And of what he feels is relevant, he will read what is interesting to him. The lesson for psychologists here, given that we do not have the machinery to saturate the government's paperwork with psychological wisdom, is that we must be interesting, relevant, and brief. We should also select targets, so that we can direct our messages. Any and every message is competing with every other one, and the larger government bureaucracies have set up defenses against the large number of messages that come in from the outside. That is, there are offices which answer correspondence that is not addressed to anyone in particular, or is addressed to too important a person, or to too large an office.

I have now discussed three psychological principles which psychologists might employ in trying to get their ideas communicated to policymakers. To review, these were the ideas of understanding the frame of reference of the policymaker, including what he accepts as evidence; recognizing what his views might be on the credibility and status of the source; and finally simply getting his attention and holding it long enough to get your message across. You can undoubtedly think of other psychological principles that might also be useful to take into account.

I will now devote the rest of this talk to urging you to devote more of your time to studying social problems. I say this, fully realizing that some of you are devoting all of your time to such problems. I realize that there are over 1,000 members of the Society for the Psychological Study of Social Issues, and that they turn out a fine journal which is devoted to the discussion and analysis of such problems. We can be proud of that, and be confident that it is doing some good. There are also probably well over one hundred psychologists in the U.S. who are working on projects which seem to be related to disarmament and international relations, and that is very encouraging, too, even though I do not find too much evidence that their findings are being used by policymakers in government, and this is perhaps for some of the reasons I am suggesting. Finally, we have the fact that about 21% of civilian psychologists[1] are working in government, which includes 8% in the federal government. This could be encouraging or not, depending on what they are working for in government, and why. Incidentally, in comparison with 8% of psychologists, about 3-3/4% (2.5 out of 67 million) of the total working force is in the federal government, not including persons in uniform.

There are less encouraging figures. The total amount of money spent on scientific research in this country was close to $16 billion in 1961, or about 3% of our gross national product. Of this, the federal government supported some $9 billion, or more than half. But in these fairly impressive totals, social science research of all kinds amounts to only 3% of the national total, and 2% of the federal government total. And social science here refers to "any study which seeks, directly or indirectly, to advance or to utilize knowledge of the behavior of human beings -- singly, in groups, or in conjunction with machines." My guess is that it includes about one-fourth psychological research, both basic and applied. As an aside: I found it interesting that although the Department of Defense commits a total of more than $24 million annually for a wide variety of social science research, this is still only 12% of all federal monies allocated to social science research, while the total Defense Department budget is approximately equal to the combined budgets of all other federal agencies. This means that Defense probably has the lowest relative rate of support for social science research in the entire government, even though the amount is absolutely quite great.[2]

Now if we can assume that 3% of all research is a relatively small fraction to be devoted to social science research in this country, and that psychology represents probably only a quarter of all social science research, it seems to me we can conclude that psychological research just is not very high in priority in this country (and probably others too; I have no non-U.S. figures). What are the reasons? Certainly our culture is partly responsible, both for the relatively small emphasis on psychological research, and indirectly for the small number of psychologists who are available to do the research. But there is a possible corollary to this finding, and that is that psychology itself has drifted to some extent out of the mainstream of the research problems that interest the culture. One piece of evidence that this has been the trend is that whereas since before the Second World War American annual expenditures for research of all kinds has increased by 50 times (from $300 million to $15 billion) membership in the APA has increased by less than 8 times during the same period (2, 500 in 1939 to 19, 000 in 1961). These figures may have resulted from a number of irrelevant factors, but they are the only figures I could find for the present.

Actually, it may not really be too important, for present purposes, to be certain whether or not psychology has been drifting away from important social problems. The important thing, from my standpoint, is to encourage you to become more interested in working on such problems, regardless of the direction of the trend. Nonetheless it does seem to me that during the past 40 years psychology, in becoming more theoretical, analytic, empirical and especially experimental, has lost some of its original, and I believe its ultimate, excuse for being. It seems to me that during the first quarter of this century many people who called themselves psychologists also considered themselves experts on social injustice, war, revolution, and crime, for example, as well. And to a large extent they were. I do not think they read any more or thought any more than we do, but I wonder if they did not study social problems -- as a professional matter -- more than do psychologists as a rule today. I strongly suspect that they did in fact read more outside their fields than we do today, both in general and about particular social problem areas. For one thing, there was less to read in those days, both in psychology and outside.

But as psychology became "modern" and "scientific, " a number of things happened.  Much of its moved to the laboratory in its pursuit of better-controlled situations, subjects and observations.  It also developed a self-generating literature which has now reached such proportions that no single psychologist can keep us with all of his field.  And finally, insofar as psychology has pursued generalizations about broad classes of behavior, it has necessarily paid less attention to the historical case, including current events.

It seems to me that this divergence may have resulted in psychologists being less well prepared today to attack social problems than they used to be.  And they may even be less well prepared to attack these problems than some contemporary non-psychologists.

Try to consider objectively the actual substantive knowledge we mastered in the course of becoming psychologists and remaining psychologists.  Consider what we read during the six or eight years we spent in colleges and graduate schools; Freud, Adler, Jung and the neo-Freudians; the Blum, Mullahy and Monroe exegeses of the preceding; Guthrie, Tolman, Hull, Spence, Skinner, and Hebb; Heider, Cooley, Mead, Newcomb, Lewin, and Festinger; Allport and Allport; Homans; Krechevski and Crutchfield; Parsons; Murray; Osgood; Feigl; Murphy.  These and others were the classics we mastered like Talmudic scholars.  There were also statistics, methodology and language requirements.  In general, did not we learn how to study problems rather than to solve them?  In general, what do we know that others, who did not read the books we did, or conduct the experiments we did, do not know?

I have read many articles, by both behavioral scientists and non-behavioral scientists, that imply or state that if only behavioral scientists would study certain problems it would be a good thing.  It is suggested that government, or humanity has much to learn from us.  I wonder if it is not more the case that humanity would benefit if anyone competent studied these problems -- be he lawyer, politician, historian, economist, political scientist, or even physicist.  The important thing is that they be studied, by careful, competent, concerned people, but regardless of discipline.

This is not to say that psychology does not have something unique to offer.  But I would suggest that although we do not like to admit it freely, our mental capacities are not necessarily superior to those of analysts in other fields.  There are no a priori reasons why we, sitting back in our chairs, can come up with better analyses than can equivalently endowed economists, theologians or bureaucrats.  Furthermore, to the extent that we psychologists have become more divorced from major social events and currents than have some of our colleagues in related fields, then to that extent we may actually have some catching up to do before we can do as good a job as our colleagues can in attacking a given, specific problem.  There may be a range of vital, social problems, including disarmament and international relations, with regard to which the psychologist may initially have to do more work than say a political scientist, historian, or journalist.  Having done his extra homework on a particular problem, however, I would hope and expect that the psychologist would then be in a superior position to contribute to solving the problem.

Now, about the problems themselves: I want to present very strongly to you my feeling that time is running out on Western civilization, and that if we are going to preserve what we think is good about it, we must act in this generation. There are forces in the world today which are inexorable. The "population explosion" is a trite phrase, but is is an understatement. It means mass starvation, mass disease, mass unemployment, mass illiteracy, and mass depletion of resources -- not only depletion of natural resources like water and fuel, but also space, places to live, and also resources like teachers and doctors and engineers. This generation was simply caught off guard by the human demands that it should and must face. On the top of the problems of plain mass human misery, arises the fact of growing, mass discontent. The poorer two-thirds of mankind may be illiterate, but they are becoming increasingly aware that their misery is not inevitable, and that a better life is possible. In reaching for this better life, they may choose a number of directions, some we cannot even foresee. Some peoples may choose to grow up gradually, under Western tutelage, and inspiration, but I suspect they will be exceptions. Because the West is such a convenient scapegoat, if for no other reason, I suspect we may more often turn out to be perceived as villains than models. One thing is certain, and that is that regardless of its humanistic intentions, the rich third of the world has not as yet shown itself able to solve the problems of the poorer two-thirds.

One could speculate that even though it would be immoral and inhumane in the extreme to do so, all this might still amount to a viable situation for Western civilization if only the lid could be held on by brute strength -- say by military force. But technology has made even this impossible. Just on the basis of reading the newspapers over the past 20 years, is there any doubt that nuclear and other weapons of mass destruction will -- if present trends continue -- be generally available throughout the world in our lifetime? I think there is no doubt. And not only will technology soon make it possible for extremely discontented people throughout the world to bring about mass violence, suffering and death, it has even now left even the superpowers with somewhat less influence than in the past. Although handfuls of men in the U.S. and USSR hold the physical survival of the Western World in their hands, and could certainly deal militarily with any given nation on earth, they are unable to "deliver" or coerce even their allies in international relations, much less each other. And this trend seems to be becoming greater, rather than less. One is possibly left with the feeling that the major powers would have more actual political power if their absolute physical power were reduced.

This description I have given you is one of present-day trends which will not go away if we do not look at them. The forces which are at work are primarily those of biology, technology and geography. We, as psychologists and as citizens who value our nation and our civilization, must come to terms with the problems I have just outlined, and others equally pressing.

At this point, let me introduce two related assumptions which underlie this discussion. The first is that for practical purposes this nation, along with other modern nations, now has a relatively fixed pool of research people to devote to problems. Some proportion of these people can and must be left free to develop and pursue very fundamental lines of inquiry which provide, in the long run, the essence of human knowledge. Yet there is another group which must be persuaded to break away and work on the short-range problems the society faces. Without a good share of the former group we become a nation of technicians and improvisers with no basis for that ever expanding knowledge of ourselves and our universe upon which we hope to base our future civilization. But without the second group of activists we run the real and present danger of losing -- for some indeterminate period -- the very institutions and society we all live in. I very strongly suspect that today the ratio of basic to applied social scientists is too high with respect to certain applied problems our society must solve in order to survive. In other words, we have to sacrifice some future knowledge to present needs.

By this time I hope I have given you a feeling of urgency about several social problems, and a sense that in order to solve them we might have to divert some of our finite, problem-solving resources. Let me now offer some intellectual rationalizations about why such diversions of resources might even be beneficial for psychology, and finally I will wind up with the suggestion that you study things you are mad about.

First, it seems to me that psychologists have mastered rather well the art of producing psychology. We have found the pool of variables worthy of study to be virtually infinite in scope, and if we tire of considering new sources of variance, we can always fall back on replicating each other's studies and criticizing each other's methodology. This is to say that we have found no limits either to the observations we can make of our universe, or to the ways in which we can conceptualize them. I am not suggesting that each individual psychologist is not guided in his efforts by his interests, his resources, and the existing fund of knowledge in the field; what I am saying is that no matter which way he goes the psychologist seems to be able to produce psychology. And this fact might lead the field to wander endlessly and aimlessly. Thus, my perhaps somewhat oversimplified view of the world is that scientific knowledge is a function of what scientists choose to investigate. And of course it follows that psychological knowledge is a function of what psychologists choose to investigate.

Now in a safe, stable world, with adequate supplies of problem-solvers, it would probably be reasonable for psychologists to study anything they chose. But the fact is there are a wide variety of problems which must be solved rather quickly, and there are too few people to solve them.

A reasonable question for psychologists to ask is What would happen to psychology if a significant number of us became more involved in current social problems. What would happen? Suppose half of the members of the APA decided to take ten years off and devote themselves only to the study of poverty, intolerance, illiteracy, apathy, international relations, crime, and social injustice in the world today. The benefit to the world of suddenly having an additional 10,000 bright, dedicated problem-solvers working in these areas would be enormous. But what about psychology? Would it not degenerate to a hodge-podge of case studies and social protest? Surely our scholarly journals would become thinner at first. But this does not mean that our defectors would have ceased to be scholars. I do not envision a dissenting mob, but rather a large number of scholarly crusaders. And though the number of studies of privileged college students and other middle class Americans would go down, these would hopefully be replaced by studies which would yield large amounts of data and insights on far larger sectors of our world than we now have. And if psychologists found themselves floundering for a time without theories, without hypotheses, and without some of the rigor they would desire, would that not really be a sign that our concern in these areas was long overdue? If we do not have theories and insights and data which are directly relevant to the pressing problems of our times, I suggest that we should. Certainly not many people would argue that there is something inherent in the field of psychology which prohibits us from having such theories, data and insights. And I think if it takes a little floundering to get them, that is simply a necessary price we should be glad to pay for bringing our field up to date.

I think at this point anyone has a perfect right to ask if I am not urging psychologists to do something they are in fact already doing. After all, in 1962 only 37% of psychologists were in universities and they were supposedly carrying out the major part of the basic research in the field and teaching the next generation of psychologists. The remainder were out in the world, possibly working on the very problems I am claiming they are not working on. And of those in the colleges and universities, are not the large majority engaged in substantive areas which are directly relevant to social problems? -- in educational psychology, in mass communication, in studies of delinquency, mental illness, public opinion and attitude change, to name just a few. Finally, as Stevenson and Teeple have pointed out in their recent survey of Research in Arms Control and Disarmament, 1960-1963, [3] "the most active group in 'peace research' has been psychologists, followed by economists, political scientists, sociologists, and physical scientists."

It may in fact be the case that psychologists are already quite involved in these current social problems. That is good. But the problems are getting worse, rather than better. I said a moment ago that what I am urging you to do is to become more involved; now I am going so far as to suggest you might try some different approaches, to become more focussed on specific social problems even though it might initially involve breaking with traditional conceptions and evidence. The important thing for us as participants in Western civilization is that the problems be solved, regardless of approach. It will take bright, dedicated people with interest and insight, and psychologists are just such people.

I have just finished reading a collection of papers which were written for the Office of Naval Research under the direction of Professor Ithiel de Sola Pool. The title of the report is "Social Science Research and National Security."[4] The papers are written by prominent social scientists, and deal with the contributions social science might make to understanding a variety of phenomena: alliances, communication of military postures among nations, producing intelligence, the role of military organizations in developing countries, the social and military implications of population growth, and internal war. Finally there is a paper on gaming as a military research procedure. These papers have in common that they point out how social science could or should be used, the implications being that it is not. They also are unanimous in not mentioning a need for social scientists to engineer any particular projects. In other words, the authors say -- and substantiate with long bibliographies -- that social scientists have much to say that is relevant to particular topics; they also outline approaches to further research. But no one mentions the possibility of assigning to social scientists a responsibility for solving problems. It may be argued that this is only proper -- that social scientists are scientists, not politicians or bureaucrats. I disagree. I say social science, and psychology in particular, has a moral responsibility to be more than a "possible source of insight."

One of the authors suggests that social science research be supported more in general, and that social scientists be left to decide on their own research subjects. The danger this author sees is that the federal government will increasingly divert more psychologists into contract research on specific problems with which the government is grappling, with the result that the training of more social scientists and, above all, the undirected search for new concepts and propositions, will suffer. As you might expect, I disagree with this insofar as psychologists working on applied problems are at all effective, and insofar as the problems need solving. My real fear is that psychologists are being bought for a price to work on projects they are not interested in, and that no one will pay attention to, and that the problems are the wrong ones to begin with. I am saying it is not the fact of working on applied projects that is wrong, but the nature of the projects, how the psychologist is used, what he learns, and what he does with what he learns. And you will recall I certainly agree that some research must always be undirected. On the other hand I do not agree with the recommendation that we psychologists simply be given time and money to solve the problems that must be solved this decade. This presupposes a degree of faith in psychology that the dispenser of money does not have. Look at it even from your own standpoint: would you accept on faith the suggestion by a group of graduate students, who had an approach you did not understand, that they would solve your problems? I think not. We all need to be convinced.

Let me add that for me the most useful paper in this volume was an analysis by Harry Eckstein of internal war -- rioting, rebellions, coups, revolutions, and the like. He disclaimed that it was a research paper, and offered it as an approach to the study of the subject. Nonetheless, it is to my knowledge the best study we have on this subject. His data base -- as we say -- was 30 books, 6 articles, and the New York Times Index. I do not know how long it took him to put his ideas together, but he questions more common assumptions on this subject per page than I have seen elsewhere, and he supports his questions with rather simple data -- newspaper data. The paper bears directly on the approach of the U. S. government to problems of revolution, subversion, and guerrilla warfare. It is by no means definitive, and it is essentially non-theoretical. But for me it is a timely, head-on attack which essentially exposes all of the major theories of revolution and violent social change to the light of some existing evidence. The next step will be to study the revolutions at hand in the same straightforward, objective manner.

It is often said that a major asset of the psychologist is his ability to replace intuition and common sense -- that is, conventional and usually implicit concepts, hypotheses, and beliefs -- with new and more sophisticated concepts and tested hypotheses. But sometimes this replacement may happen too soon, and I think this may be one of the reasons the replacements are not readily accepted by non-psychologists. It seems to me that the most important first steps in an investigation is to understand thoroughly the conventional wisdom, the common sense concepts, intuitions and beliefs. In the first place the conventional wisdom has in a very practical sense worked for those people who are most involved. And maybe in fact their wisdom constitutes a fairly good theory. But furthermore, even if the conventional wisdom is not very good, it will continue to be used, even after the psychologist has replaced it in his own journals with more sophisticated concepts, unless the psychologist either convinces the people who are involved that the new perspectives are good ones, or else replaces the people with himself.

To conclude: What should we study? I have named some key areas: war, revolution, crime, poverty, illiteracy, disease, complacency, apathy, security, social injustice. What I want us to study are things we think are important to society. I want us to study what we as citizens think is important. I want us to study things that make us angry when we read the newspapers. I do not want our studies to be biased by our anger, although we could have a long discussion about how fear of emotion leads to the study of emotionless -- and therefore, by definition, unimportant -- problems. But rather let our concern and our anger lead us to attack big problems and to try to understand them at a human level. Then we can apply our traditional theories and understandings as we think they are applicable. But let us begin more of our studies with the approach that says, "This is a deplorable situation; how can it be made better?" And use your own standards of what you mean by better. They may not be true in any absolute sense, but they are as good as anyone else's.

We face a world today with which existing institutions are showing themselves inadequate to deal. Nuclear technology and modern weapons are spreading precisely as the prophets of doom said they would. Populations are exploding in the hungry two-thirds of the world with machine-like precision. There is mass misery and mass unrest.

There is mass protest against centuries of injustice even in our midst. There will be more unrest as more of the miserable peoples of the world come to realize their misery is not necessarily God's will. And these miserable people, that the fortunate, powerful people in the world have not found the means to teach reading, writing and arithmetic, have more importantly not been taught democratic values, nor have they experienced them. Their demands, aided by modern weapons, may be disorderly indeed.

There is no natural law that says our universities, as we know them, are adequate to train people to understand and deal with these problems. But faced with the necessity for change, what will we do? Will we continue to climb academic ladders, and to generate research within relatively ineffective institutions, and to search for contracts and grants not necessarily of our own choosing? I hope not. I want us to spend more long days and nights worrying about the ultimate problems of mankind, because these are now our immediate applied problems. And if worrying and studying these problems is not the way to climb within our institutional hierarchies, and to achieve positions of power and influence, I suggest that in that case the hierarchies, and the power structure within which status in them results in power, may not be worth climbing in.

Let me end on an empirical note. I image everyone in this room has at least one research project under way. I would like to ask you -- for all of our information -- how many of you consider your current research is directly relevant to a social problem that you feel strongly about? Now, of those who feel you are working on important social problems -- war, poverty, disease, illiteracy, vice, social injustices, apathy, complacency, birth control -- how many have a pretty clear idea of how your research could be used to improve the situation?

Do you have an idea who will consider using it, or when or where its use is likely?

I think this show of hands is interesting. We should bear in mind that we are psychologists in the Capital area who are interested in getting up on Saturday morning to hear a symposium on international relations.

With that, I rest my case.

### Footnotes

1. 5% of psychologists are in uniform.
2. Figures on social science research are from "Special Analysis: The Federal Government In Behavioral Science: Fields, Methods, and Funds, " (William W. Ellis, Study Director) Published and Distributed by the American Enterprise Institute for Public Policy Research, 1012 Fourteenth Street, N. W., Washington, D. C. 20005. (The statement "88th Congress -- Second Session, Report No. 4 -- May 11, 1964" is printed on

this report, so it may appear in the Congressional Record.)

3. Eric Stevenson and John Teeple, <u>Research in Arms Control and Disarmament</u>, 1960-1963, dated September 30, 1963. The report lists no publisher or address, but states that Stevenson and Teeple are "Consultants" to the International Affairs Program of the Ford Foundation.

4. Ithiel de Sola Pool and others, "Social Science Research and National Security." A Report Prepared by the Research Group in Psychology and the Social Sciences, Smithsonian Institution, Washington, D. C., Under Office of Naval Research Contract. March 5, 1963. Copies are available to "qualified requesters" from DDC (Defense Document Center), Washington 25, D. C. Foreign announcement and dissemination not authorized.

# POLITICAL INVENTION AS A STRATEGY AGAINST WAR

Gardner Murphy
The Menninger Foundation

Within the last few days it has been brought home to me, very vividly, that this or any other little contribution I might try to make, is likely to be useful only if we are serious about developing a very broad interdisciplinary, and international, approach to our problem. I believe political invention to be of profound importance, or I should not take your time with it. But its importance lies in its close articulation with the psychological, economic, historical, military, anthropological, sociological, and other specialized approaches. It is the predicament of man that the many approaches to his plight cannot do the job. Only a new integration can do that.

The word "invention" is often limited to the production of material appliances. One speaks of the invention of printing, or of the incandescent bulb; one does not speak of the invention of the sonnet, or of square dancing, or of religious toleration, or of political democracy. Yet invention is not really the incorporation of an idea in a thing; the embodiment of an idea in a highly specific material object serving a highly specific purpose. This curious usage has blinded us to the staggering importance of social inventions which occur all around us. It gives us the feeling that inventions just don't happen explicitly and purposefully in the matter of the social domain; rather, they grow like Topsy. Whether suddenly or rapidly, they are regarded as the expressions of capricious, impersonal, inevitable processes over which there can be no ultimate control. At a time in history to which invention, of the specific sort required to combat human destruction, is so desperately necessary, we do not even have a word to name what it is that we need. We are dealing with a class of political inventions; indeed political inventions are at the apex of a pyramid of inventions which we need. Representative government, for example, must develop in various ways in order to be flexible enough, and quick enough to respond to some of the overnight threats that are looming upon us.

And to generalize some of the words of the sociologist of fifty years ago, we need not only inventions, we need an awareness of the process of inventing inventions. Just as the small boy in Western culture becomes aware at eight or ten years of age of the process of invention, becomes aware that somebody invented telegraphy, and that many are involved in inventing television improvements, American youth needs to be aware that there is such a thing as inventing political institutions. There needs to be respect for the complexity, the flexibility, the need to protect such inventions, the need for a large area of freedom and flexibility; the need for the kinds of attributes which enter into such flexibility; the need for tolerance of those whose inventive ideas are ninety-nine per cent wild and unworkable, for the sake of those who can produce an occasional idea that leads to electrifying new possibilities. There needs to be an understanding that there must be a basic science if there is to be an applied science. There must be principles of nature and of human life that are clearly apprehended if there are to be experimental innovations worthy of receiving the name "invention." There must be a community ready to respect the social and political inventor, and a community capable of flexible selection, adaptation, integration of such inventions.

I think our modern excitement about creativity is, perhaps, of a little help to us here, for "creativity" is a term which pulls together the various arts and sciences under one rubric, and makes it evident that social, moral, religious, political inventions may depend on much the same basic psychology as that of what we call creativeness in the arts and sciences. It may be that a slow maturing of our understanding of man as a political animal is dawning upon us, as we glimpse the possibility that many of the same psychological laws appear when we are creating can openers and when we are creating world states. I am sure you have sat, as I have, countless times, before the loud speaker or the television screen, and listened to wise and helpful analyses of world politics and international affairs, in which copious and flexible awareness of human history is combined with a sensitive appreciation of the personalities of political leaders, great and small. At the same time, I am sure you have suffered, as I have, in the feeling that the whole tissue is one of impressions and opinions, where solid and replicable facts are hard to come by. Indeed, the absence of experimental method on the one hand and the possibility of measurement on the other hand, doom the speaker, in the midst of all his wisdom, to flimsy predictions and vague open horizons beyond which anything may turn out to be true. There is, in other words, no possibility of importing into the discussion the way of the inventor -- the clean, firm, confrontation of the problem. What is it that the inventor wants to make? What are the possible raw materials? How would they have to be selected, treated, developed, put together? How would the pretests have to be made? I do not say that all inventors go through these processes in the same way, but I do say that in many careful studies, such as those of J. J. Rossman, it becomes plain that invention is an art based upon a system of interrelated areas of knowledge and an orderly and disciplined conception of the way in which the details can be worked into a totality. There are even cases like that of Benjamin Franklin, in which identically the same psychological attributes went into the invention of a stove, an almanac, and a political system.

Social inventiveness is, of course, rich, complex, and universal. What it lacks is explicitness, dignity, social encouragement, and awareness of its indispensable role -- in fact, its central position in the sciences which can preserve the continuity of a man's life. To plead for research exemplifying the value of social inventiveness would be childish and sterile, for almost everything in the world of practical affairs, as well as almost everything in the world of social science, pays mute tribute to the hand of this type of inventor. What is needed, rather, is the awareness of what these inventors have in common, awareness of what all innovators and social inventors can properly aspire to achieve, as they become "inventors of world unity." Political

science can no longer remain just a study of ways in which political
life goes on, since patently, if it goes on in the present way much longer
there will be no more political life.  Rather, it must invent itself out of
old forms and into new ones, in the explicit recognition that political invention, like all social invention, is embodied in individuals, groups,
techniques, purposes; that it is capable of specification, measurement,
and experimental control.  This is the task to which we must set our
hand.

Invention is a kind of skill, and I hope to show that like all
skills, it depends on the application of a science.  The possibilities of
developing a basic science relating to political skills may take either a
deductive or an inductive direction, and perhaps when both paths have
been followed a while, they may prove to intersect.  Among deductive
possibilities, we may consider the logical possibilities relating to the
basic types of political interactions, defined in terms of observed time
and space attributes, functional and purposive properties, sharpness of
differentiation of roles, and also of the personalities carrying out each
role.  Some of the classical rules relating to the dispersion of social
effects from a center to a fringe, on the analogy of ripples in a pool,
may be compared with instrumental views in which each member of the
group is achieving a goal or a sub-goal, in terms of the organization of
his wants, and the groups are classified not only with respect to their
ultimate goals, but their subdivision into groups pursuing contrary or
incompatible goals.  There is no need to develop all the possible forms
of classification of intra or inter-group activities, but only to make
clear that such classification must be reasonably comprehensive and
cover all logically identifiable possibilities, if the leadership skills,
especially of a political order, are to be sharply perceived as possibilities for future development.  No one is likely to invent incandescent
bulbs by randomly trying all metals; even the indefatigable Edison
started with a finite number of possible filament materials.  He who
undertakes to define new types of political skills that can be invented,
must know something about the archeology of the Mayas, the clan structure of the Scottish highlands, the methods of rewarding petty political
favors as practiced in the Greek city states, the principles governing
the selection of Panchayats in ancient and in modern India, as well as
the effects of industrialization upon cracker-barrel philosophy in a
Tennessee hamlet during the development of the Tennessee Valley
Authority.

With this type of illustration we have clearly passed from the
deductive possibilities to the inductive possibilities.  The important
thing is that the twain shall meet.  We might even visualize an encyclopedia of group relationships, finding a place for the simplest and the
most complex, the most static and the most volatile, the most traditional and the most subject to individual innovation.  When we develop
such an encyclopedia we shall certainly find something like Mendeleyev's
periodic table of elements.  We shall find that certain types of group
relationships give rise to certain qualitatively distinct types of emerging political response.  And here and there we shall be able to predict
the discovery of a missing element; that is, we shall be able to invent

a new type of political leadership. As with Mendeleyev, we shall be able to predict, but only by having a germ of a theory, not merely by using a compounding of measures. We shall, in other words, have to be fully deductive and fully inductive at the same time if we are to get seriously into the business of inventing ways of studying the process of inventing.

But will the development of a science of political leadership automatically provide the basis for political skills? We all know, in our sober moments, that even knowledge and wisdom cannot suffice. Statecraft is a complicated skill, one of the highest of the arts. Now skill is specific. Socrates was one of the wisest of men, but a poor sculptor. Our problem in this last half of the Twentieth Century far transcends the problem of acquiring knowledge about human beings and their environment. Even on the part of the wisest of men who lovingly assess each bit of information, each new outlook, there must come in- to existence a special art, or skill, based indeed upon science, but transcending science exactly as surgery transcends the knowledge of anatomy, and the paintings of Leonardo da Vinci transcend the knowl- edge of paints and brushes. The skill of a statesman transcends all that is known of politics and war in any given era.

Am I then pleading that there will always remain a large unre- solved component, a tertium quid which transcends control? No, I am pleading for the development of a new kind of political skills based on knowledge and wisdom, but also upon inductive experimental studies of political skills whereon we base the emerging new social and politi- cal sciences. I am suggesting that we cannot even clearly see our way to this third level of understanding and control with respect to war, because we are still thinking diffusely and dreamily about human reali- ties which have not yet been well faced, realities which have to do with the special skills of human adjustment at all levels, whether at the level of family, community, state, or world order. I am suggesting that science, moving so massively through the physical and biological realms, and now within recent years, aspiring to a definition of the laws which govern societies, laws which can be observed, verified, and even to some degree experimented upon and remade into more satisfying, higher developments, can and must lead into laws relating to those total integrations which mean the difference between peace and war.

Will these laws then be simply an extension of the present social sciences? I think not. The social sciences are themselves specialty problems, facets, chips from a complex and massive reality. It is quite likely, for example, that a great deal that is at the very depths of human nature, and which is not even glimpsed by our knowledge today, will tomorrow be an important part of our sociology, our ethics, and our international relations. It is quite possible that cross-cultural studies of anthropological problems will show interactions between bio- logical and social realities in man which give new types of perspective, will make possible the emergence of new leaders, and will thereby bring into play the social and political skills which have never been effective in the past. It is possible, for example, that the art of leadership in small or large groups, and that the art of reconciliation of conflicting human groups, will take on forms which cannot well be extrapolated from the limited group dynamics of today, but will prove, within a new political system, to supply just the working technique which will make the difference between the destruction and the preservation of life.

You may well ask whether we can hope for so different a kind of skill to emerge for us so quickly, whether in a situation as desperate as that which we face today, we can expect totally new insights as to political leadership to emerge in a flash. The only honest way I can answer such a question is to ask whether we are really seriously working at this problem, and how fast we can move, if we wish. Very specifically, what are we doing in the teaching of social leadership skills? What kinds of leadership know-how and political know-how are taught in our psychology, our sociology, our group dynamics, our brainstorming, our executive and industrial research studies? Over my desk come each year dozens of earnest little studies of small group effects. Here and there a big caliber idea has emerged, maybe one or two per decade. The trouble is that you and I, as well as the political leaders at the top and the semi-illiterate political leaders who gather local votes for all sorts of local purposes, are not really beginning to think in terms of the central issue, which is this: How, by using the utmost of information and wisdom, can we move on to research upon the ways of controlling and preventing catastrophe? I am not pleading for abandoning the existing array of social science studies in the prevention of war, because I think they are the best we have. I think something new must be added and I shall attempt to say what it is. I shall now attempt to show what I think the possibilities may be for research on political skills related to the prevention of war, directed primarily to those in whose hands fateful decisions are likely to lie. I refer to studies already going on.

First, I will mention the extraordinary Stanford studies of the causation of war, as seen in the mature and rational integrations of economic, political, and psychological knowledge. With great historical and political sophistication, they have managed to give us a panorama of historical perspective on the first world war. After it reached a certain high level of complexity and sophistication it moved, of course, into the world of computers. You are dealing with such vast quantities of information that you must find a way to code and program your information, teach your computer how to do what you want it to do, and derive a multi-dimensional picture of the particular circumstances that were channeled through the mind and heart of William II of Germany, Lord Gray, Raymond Poincaré, and a dozen others, resulting in a massive picture which looks like predetermination. The crisis that leads to war is thus compared with crises that did not lead to war and we begin to have an almost experimental picture of historical causation. This much I can say and I yield to no one in enthusiasm for this work. Note however, that it leaves out exactly the dimension which I have tried to stress. It does indeed give the personalities of the Kaiser and Lord Gray, but it cannot give, in fully documented form, the dimensions which actually controlled the decisions. The records suggest that they were made impulsively, that there were a few hours of failing "impulse control." Even if all the information were at hand on this point, there still would be the massive question: How did the impulse structure of the Kaiser integrate in the decision process? What was the structure of the interpersonal decision process? What kind of political skill could have altered the decisions?

It is indeed, the decision process which stands out conspicuously as we try to find what is next needed. Many groups of social scientists, psychiatrists, and others have been working on this process. Some of the major studies, with large groups and great devotion, such as are available, for example, in the Center for Conflict Resolution at the University of Michigan, are exploring around the edges of this problem. It is my own hesitant thought that even these studies are too narrowly conceived. They are formulated essentially in terms of conflict. The basic issue, however, I think is not conflict -- but the social skill which transcends both conflict and integration, the science and art of transcending explosive situations, and likewise, situations of apathy, laziness, self-blame, and all of the other things related to war. In fact, without any conflict at all, there could be many types of factors leading into a situation from which there would be no escape that leaders in the modern world could find in a sort of crisis moment, a "fail safe" moment. Conflict is of enormous importance; it belongs near the heart of our study. We have, however, precariously, a few years, in the world's unstable condition, a few years in which the triangular power struggle of the United States, the Soviet Union, and mainland China, will have to be cautiously handled while we are learning something about the political skills that we do not now possess. It is your privilege to say that the problem is insoluble, and that within ten years, mainland China will be able and willing to take the incredible risks of establishing itself, if it can, as master of the world, or you may perfectly well take any other pessimistic course you like. I am saying that there is no alternative to this pessimistic outlook except the development of a new kind of political skill.

Now, actually, I am not at all pessimistic about this. I think that our difficulty has been that we have taken political skill much too lightly, or regarded it as a sort of gift of the gods, incapable of being really understood. There is a mystique, a charismatic quality about the Julius Ceasar, the Cromwell, the Napoleon, the Bismarck, the Lenin -- yes, with all our hate, even the Hitler -- that we are prone to regard as ultimately incomprehensible, irrational, in the hands of Fate's furies, or an almost personal devil.

Now, I will agree at once that I am making a special problem of a special kind of person, a political leader. Are not the same kinds of problems with us all the way down the scale, highest to the lowest? Are not the problems of human adjustment, concord and discord, understanding and blind refusal to understand, universal problems of human life? Shall we not have to have a social, political skill adequate both for the simplest and the most complex human problems? Shall we not have to develop a science, in all its richness, dealing with all the aspects of human adjustment? Yes, this is exactly what I want to say. The reason why we do not have the highest level of skill in war-prevention is that we have almost no skill at all at a scientific level anywhere with regard to this whole dimension of political leadership. We still live largely at a level of mystique, or the charismatic. We often look, for example, within the individual, disregarding the ecology, the social pressure, the complex cultural predetermination, or use bland descriptive phrases rather than dynamic clues, or look for sublimations of biological drives, rather than trying to understand the complexity of interpersonal relations. We admit the complexity of man when we look at the trouble into which he falls, but deny his complexity when we look at his learning processes. He gets into trouble at a level considerably more complex than that of a monkey, but when we study his learning processes, we go all the way down to rats and mice looking for analogies. Analogies are all right, but they remain analogies, and in the meantime we look at that narrow band of human nature that we think we understand, lying as it does in between the true biological structuring of mankind through the human gene pool and the basic gene organization which goes into each individual life. And on the other hand, we have no real skill to cope with the complexities of man's socio-cultural predetermination, hoping that somehow we shall be forgiven just because the problems are too complicated for us. We forget, moreover, that this more complex multi-dimensional picture of human nature will have to set in a time-space frame of reference with historical determination and the present ecological surroundings both keyed into the complex of stimulation acting upon individual men in the social group at any given time. We know that we are not on the right track until we have a scheme of interpersonal relations reaching all the way from genetics and bio-chemistry at one end, to the character of the visionary, the prophetic, the political genius, at the other end. We do not have a language or the concepts that are complicated enough to do justice to the facts already before us. Of course, the situation will shake down and become simplified when we understand it; this is always the case in science. It cannot be shaken down, however, until we understand it. The issue is to let in the light from every window to see as clearly as we can and later we can move over to an alcove and use the special light required for microscopic observation, but we have not yet come to that point. We shall have to understand the ecology of the political leader as well as his character.

We begin to see the emerging possibilities for a world-wide view of attitude and opinion, morale and value characterizing the peoples of the world. We begin to see something in depth regarding the understandings and misunderstandings, the flexibilities and rigidities of the patterns of world opinion, where there is case-hardened obtuseness and where there is flexibility. All the way from verbal statements of the yes-no sort down to the deepest projective level, there are possibilities of relating this tissue of attitudes and values to the geographical ecology and the socio-cultural dynamics of each group.

This will lead, of course, far beyond the scope of the observational techniques of today. If we wish to understand the patterns and

tides of world opinion and valuation, we shall have to use the more re-
fined techniques of the experimental psychology, if and when critical
tests of each hypothesis can be made. We shall have to study the techniques of scanning and searching for reality as they have developed in
the psychological laboratory in recent years, and will have to relate
them to the problem of perceptual defense, the warping of external
reality by needs and fears, and study the steps by which a person im-
prisoned within such subjective self-deception can be led back again
to better reality testing. And self-deception will have to be seen in
relation not only to the individual, but to the group-life and the international life, as Morton Deutsch has so well shown.

This again leads into systematic study of communication skills
from simple dyadic intercommunication of two persons, to the most
complex conversational or jury or parliamentary or professional group
interactions, with suitable content analysis of meanings and with the
study of para-language and kinesics, to set the whole communication
process in its fullest perspective, sweeping out irrationalities which
clog the decision-making processes, and at a deeper level, showing
the positive contribution which each person in the group setting is capable of making. Ithiel Pool at Massachusetts Institute of Technology has
already pointed the way, while Anatol Rapaport has shown the role of
risk-taking in the war games type of situation, and Systems Development Corporation have introduced emotional distorting factors, along
with sheer information factors, in guiding quick decisions.

You see, I did not want to leave you with the idea that I am
pleading, rather vacuously, for a type of research that has not been
done. What I am pleading for is the recognition of the vast importance
of the many fragmentary, little clues that we have today, appealing to
you to recognize that we are already passing into the social science
analysis of war, and moving into the third stage which is the study of
those political and social skills which can actually implement a war-
less world. Able men have already been erecting a scaffold for a
fresh beginning at a level never previously entertained. My role here,
as I plead for research on a significant kind of war prevention, is to
point out that many vital, though scattered beginnings are already
available.

There is, moreover, the study of political personalities, both
by autobiography, by interview, by projective test approaches, which
has several times been successfully done. There is even the study of
personalities at long distance, as in the wartime studies of the personality of Adolf Hitler, designed by some Washington agencies to
probe into the weak spots, the shattering regions which might be so
activated from a distance, so as to cause a crack-up. There is even
the brilliant suggestion of Dean White of Mills College, that by docu-
mentary analysis, and socio-cultural studies of context, we may verify
hypotheses about the motivation of political leaders now long since
dead, and set up hypotheses for future contingencies which can actually
be tested by such techniques. The biographer and the literary critic
have, of course, long since told us how to make assured inference as
to what motivated some character from long ago and pointed out docu-

mented techniques of consolidating such an opinion. But I think perhaps none until the last few years, has realized the richness of possible cross-checking offered by using very large amounts of material and by coding and computer techniques for the verification of such hypotheses. I do quite seriously believe, with the ancient Pythagoreans, that there is a certain rationality about numbers which not only makes for verification of that which was at first only dimly guessed, but may look for replication, for the uniformities of nature upon which lawfulness and intelligibility can ultimately depend. I do, therefore, quite seriously believe that by combining this with all the other methods we have used, we are coming into an era of personality study, which both in its own right, its own light, and as a key to the understanding of war, may play a part in revitalizing the study of man.

One of the best things about the approach is that its empirical aspects can be tested. As the Sherifs have shown, they may actually build the conflict situation into a reconciliation situation by the study of supraordinate goals shared by all. I would weave the Sherif technique, the Ithiel Pool technique, the Anatol Rapaport technique, the Robert North technique, and many others into the tightest and strongest cable that I knew how to contrive. The red thread at the center of this great cable will be the conception of the research-ability, the experiment-ability, of the phenomenon of social and political leadership.

Now, in the matter of political skills, we must entertain hypotheses to be tested. Indeed, we must take much of what Kirtly Mather calls "outrageous hypotheses" and we must systematically test these by the methods of a forward-looking history; that is, by the Stanford methods I mentioned above, and by a combination of other empirical, and indeed experimental, methods. We must make maps of the future -- what Nathan Israeli calls a "museum of the future," and we must begin to live in this museum. Examples of five outrageous hypotheses are these: (1) Within ten years computer technology will have taken over the content and the method of the social sciences, and no problem will be a meaningful problem for the social sciences unless it can be computerized. This will change the whole structure and meaning of social science. (2) There will result from this a school of psychological politics where people will learn the kind of psychological politics that the computers can understand, and the problems of which they can sit and solve. (3) There will come, at the content level, what I shall call United States reactionary sagacity, by which I mean that the consistency of the reactionary position can and will predominate over the looseness of liberal systems. Barry Goldwater will seem like a flaming liberal when the inevitable case-hardened reaction takes shape in this computerized, efficient, slick, and ultra-modern form. (4) But there are others who can do this better with the incredible skill with which the Chinese Marxists are remaking society, they will move into political inventiveness with all the consistency of a completely thorough, and if you like paranoid, or at any rate systematic Marxism, and they will vastly outdo the political inventiveness of all the rest of us. I believe this will be quite evident within ten years, and well consolidated within fifteen. (5) Finally, my last proposition is that a social science elite will, nevertheless, develop everywhere, familiar with all the methods and outlooks, and that a sort of brotherhood of such an elite, even a world brotherhood, has to come. The question whether it will come before or after the supremacy of the Chinese political scientists will have to be answered.

These hypotheses are to be formulated and systematically tested by gathering data pertinent to these year by year, month by month. That is the only way in which a serious social science hypothesis of this magnitude can be tested, but there are other methods. They are, however, practically all of them quantitative, experimental, and to a large degree computerized methods.

You see then that we will get the integration that I asked for, and we can get it either in a world rebuilding or a world shattering form. I do not know whether the movements that I described are "good" or not. I am perfectly sure that they will have to be reckoned with.